AN INTRODUCTION TO ANCIENT EGYPTIAN LAWS AND PUNISHMENTS

B. A. ATKINSON

Editing, typesetting and publishing by UK Book Publishing

www.ukbookpublishing.com

ISBN: 978-1-914195-35-8

CONTENTS

ILLUSTRATIONS

FOREWORD

Angela P. Thomas, *Liverpool University*

During the last sixty years or so our knowledge of ancient Egypt has increased greatly. This has come about through archaeological excavations, through research on monuments and tombs and also material in museums, through the study and interpretation of older and more recently discovered inscriptions and texts, and through the application of scientific techniques to many items and of course to Egyptian mummies. Despite the many books and articles which have been written, this remarkable ancient civilisation continues to exert a general interest and fascination in its culture and achievements. Aspects of ancient Egyptian thought, morality and religious belief in relation to the social order, law, crime and punishment are certainly important to our understanding of Egyptian society and are more difficult to interpret and these matters are the subject of this book.

The author, Barbara Atkinson, developed an interest in ancient Egypt at a young age after seeing three illustrations of Egyptian art in a children's encyclopaedia and often visited her local museum in Newcastle-upon-Tyne to see the Egyptian material on display. Later she undertook various studies in Egyptology including evening classes in hieroglyphs at the University of Durham, an online Level 3 Diploma in Egyptology from Oxford Learning College, a number of short online courses and after three years' part-time study online received the award of the Certificate in Egyptology from the University of Manchester in 2015. She has visited

Egypt and decided to write about law, order and crime in ancient Egypt out of particular interest in these subjects.

In the book evidence from stories, texts and other sources is brought forward to reveal information about the hierarchy and order of Egyptian society, the way in which disputes might be settled, what constituted minor or serious crimes, the conduct of trials and the nature of the punishments for particular crimes. Religious beliefs were also a distinct part of the legal system. In the religious text the Book of the Dead in connection with the Judgement after Death, in one spell the deceased made a declaration usually known as the Negative Confession but which is really a confession of innocence. The deceased declared that he had done no evil and had not committed theft or killed or engaged in bad behaviour or offended the gods. However, some misdemeanours in life perhaps did not prevent a successful judgement and entry to the Egyptian Afterlife. In the case of a serious crime during life, such as the murder or attempted murder of the divine king, the punishment was most likely to be death in some form. There is the problem as to what a death sentence meant for criminals in terms of gaining access to the Afterlife or if they definitely or at least in theory were intended not to achieve this. The evidence relating to this is open to some debate and this question and others are discussed in the course of the book. There is not always a clear answer to some questions and readers will be able to consider the evidence and form their own thoughts and opinions.

Angela P. Thomas

Angela Thomas studied Egyptology at the University of Liverpool and University College London. She worked as a museum curator with Egyptian material for over 30 years and also taught evening classes on ancient Egypt for the W.E.A. Latterly until retiring she was an Honorary Teaching Fellow for 6 years at the K.N.H. Centre for Biomedical Egyptology at the University of Manchester.

ACKNOWLEDGEMENTS

There are a number of people whom I would like to acknowledge without whose help, guidance and patience I would not have been able to complete this task.

Firstly, many thanks to my husband John of nearly 50 years along with our two daughters Angela and Julie who have supported and encouraged me throughout. I also express my thanks to the following people:- Angela P. Thomas who proofread the manuscript, advising where amendments were required, patiently corrected grammar and advised the correct order of pharaonic names within cartouches, Dr. Penny Wilson with whom I study hieroglyphs and to my cousin Colin who has spent many hours assisting with hieroglyph layout.

Last but not least I wish to thank Dr. Joyce Tyldesley and Dr. Glenn Godenho, who were my tutors during the three years when I studied for The University of Manchester Certificate in Egyptology, and from where I graduated with this certificate in 2015.

I dedicate this book to our grandchildren Toni (Antonia Roberta), Mayson JD, Daniel Thomas and Bethany Elicia, all of whom have listened to 'Grommy' rant on about Egypt, Land of the Pharaohs.

PREFACE

Many books have been written about Egypt or have made reference to it on their pages, it was one such tome A. Mee's, "*The Children's Encyclopaedia*" (Vol. 1A), 1963, which fuelled my interest many years ago. At the back of the book I came across a picture of Pharaoh Siptah from Dynasty 19, buried in KV47 (Valley of the Kings), and on turning the page I looked at a scene from the Book of the Dead and a wall painting from a tomb at Gizeh [Giza]. I would turn to these pages in the encyclopaedia regularly just to look at those beautiful pictures, and I now have the time to renew my long-buried passion, with every spare moment being given up to research and study.

Ongoing projects are Middle Egyptian Hieroglyphs which I study at Durham University usually one night per week during term time under the tutelage of Dr. Penny Wilson, and I also conduct personal research into various aspects of Egyptology. 'The University of Manchester Certificate in Egyptology', a three-year online course which I graduated from in July 2015, is a venture on which I would recommend any budding Egyptologist to embark (see link).

www.egyptologyonline.manchester.ac.uk

This book which I hope you will find as enjoyable to read as I did in researching and writing it, endeavours to deal with pharaonic duties, crime, punishment and the afterlife in ancient Egypt. I am interested in many areas, but mummification and the afterlife are of prime interest, leading to my curiosity being aroused and wondering what was involved when a person committed a crime, was found guilty and punished. In ancient Egyptian mythology and belief, what happened to his or her soul?

THE COLOUR OF THE ANCIENT EMPIRES

A portrait from one of the oldest picture galleries in the world ; King Siphtah of Egypt, from the miles of painted walls and ceilings leading to the tombs in the Valley of the Kings.

Illustration 1 - Pharaoh Akhenre-Setepenre Merenptah Siptah
(Mee, A. The Children's Encyclopaedia, Vol. 1A,
Everybody's Publications Ltd., 1963, 361)

Illustration 2 - from the Book of the Dead
(Mee, A. The Children's Encyclopaedia, Vol. 1A,
Everybody's Publications Ltd., 1963, 362)

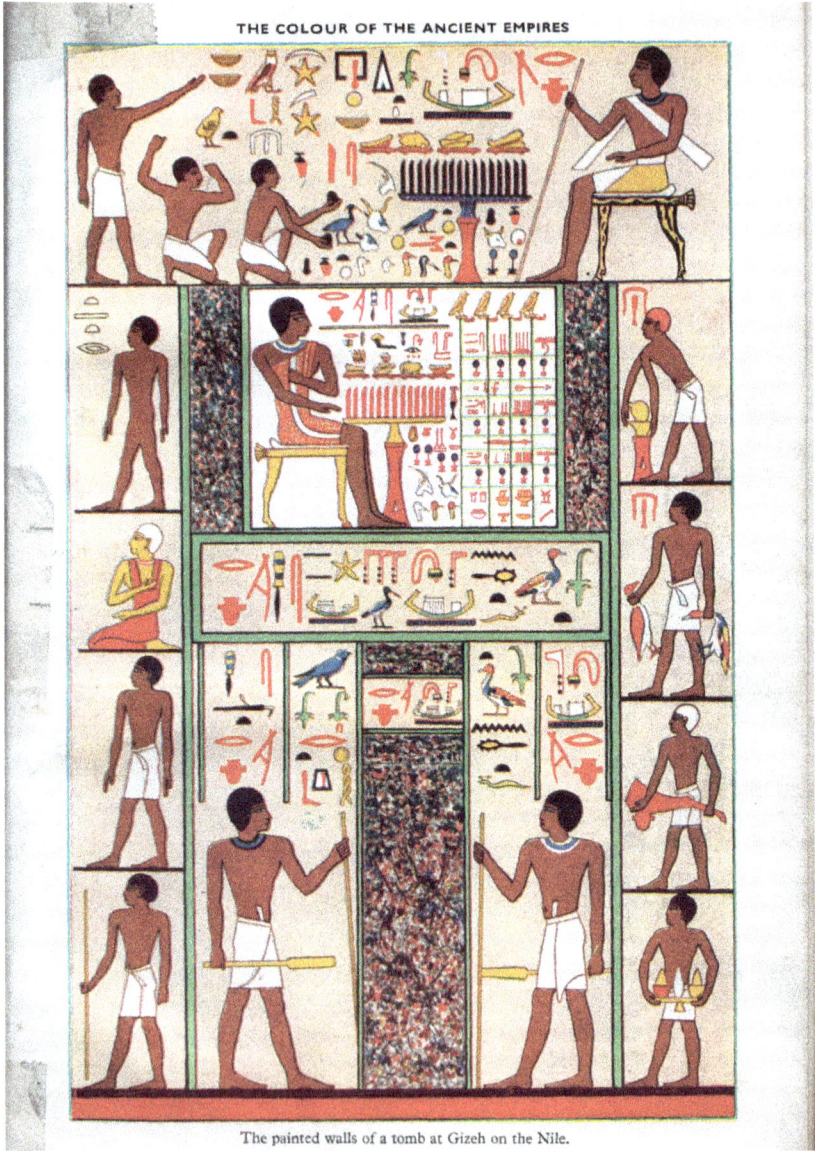

THE COLOUR OF THE ANCIENT EMPIRES

The painted walls of a tomb at Gizeh on the Nile.

Illustration 3 - Ritual scene from a tomb wall at Giza
(Mee, A. The Children's Encyclopaedia, Vol. 1A,
Everybody's Publications Ltd., 1963, 363)

CHAPTER ONE

Introduction to Ancient Egyptian Life

KEMET

The river was vital for all Egypt's requirements, such as cereals, vegetables and clothing crops. Egypt's fertile agricultural land was due to the black silt carried down during the inundation, which also gave Egypt its native name of Kemet meaning 'the Black Land.' The transportation of granite, limestone, food etc. was moved up and down the Nile on ships and barges. and the river was also used in the defence of the country by the army and navy, from its southern to its northern borders.

Although the Nile was essential to Egyptian life, it was also a very dangerous place, as it was the home of the Nile crocodile and hippopotamus. These are very dangerous animals to encounter, and whilst travelling on the river, or being in or around the waters' edge was a precarious business. There have been instances where hippopotami and crocodiles have attacked and killed ancient Egyptians whilst going about their daily chores.

At various times during its history, Egypt was a divided country, with three intermediate periods when there were separate rulers in the north and south. The first ever Pharaoh believed to have united the divided Egypt was Narmer from Dynasty 0, c.3100BC. His name was discovered in a serekh, an oblong shape in the form of what is believed to be a representation of the palace, and can be seen on the reverse side of what is known as the Narmer Palette. The serekh is the forerunner to the cartouche, both of which enclosed the Pharaoh's name and was deemed to be a protective force.

Illustration 4 - Serekh of Narmer, (Nr-mr meaning Catfish)
Author's sketch

Manetho, a third century BC Egyptian priest wrote the *Aegyptiaca* which contains a list of the Pharaohs' names in their cartouches along with their respective dynasties. There are though some omissions such as Akhenaten, Tutankhamun and Queen Hatshepsut.

Some of Egypt's most prized and well-known artefacts come from one of these unlisted Pharaohs' tombs, that of Tutankhamun in the Valley of the Kings.

Another tomb, which was discovered at the onset of World War II, also yielded exotic treasure. This belonged to a king of the 21st Dynasty, by the name of Psusennes I, the Silver Pharaoh, because of the beautifully etched silver coffin in which he was interred. Psusennes I ruled from Tanis in the north, during the Third Intermediate period, whilst the High Priests of Amun ruled in Thebes in the south. Both of these Pharaohs' tombs were virtually intact, and thankfully, for posterity, the tomb robbers missed out on two fantastic hauls.

It is thought that many thefts occurred during the closure of a tomb, and we do know that builders and workmen were very often to blame. Official documentation includes execration texts (written curses in hieratic script), decrees and contemporary accounts of state trials and local trials. We will see evidence of this within the following chapters.

A range of caches have been discovered containing small objects such as shabti, which were used to assist the deceased in the afterlife, through to large statues. Inscriptions on the shabti are written so that when the deceased are required to work, the shabti will do it for them. Some deposits were from temples, others revealed the bodies of royalty. Amongst the treasures were found magicians' boxes containing objects of their trade, articles such as papyri with written spells, prescriptions, rites and rituals for many occasions, and amulets, ivory wands and figurines. Magic was common in ancient Egypt, and was believed to have been used during the attempts on a king's life.

From the discoveries such as the king list which was discovered on the Temple wall of Seti I at Abydos, Tutankhamun's and Psusennes' treasure, mummy caches, and other findings, Egyptologists are able to build up details of time lines, relationships, funerary rites, religion and many aspects of ancient Egyptian life and death.

PHARAOH (GREAT HOUSE - ⬜) *pr ʿ3*

Pharaoh is a Greek term meaning 'great house' and was not used by the Egyptians to refer to the king, until the New Kingdom era; As we can see from the heading, this word originally referred to the palace – the great house.

Pharaoh was the most important person in Egypt, ruling the government, high priests, and in addition was seen as a living god, as noted in one of his titles "S3 Re - son of Re" He was expected to build temples in honour of the deities, and have his triumphs carved into their walls and columns, showing what a great king he was and how he revered the gods.

The temple complexes of Karnak and Luxor (ancient Thebes), are prime examples of pharaonic architecture, where many Pharaohs depicted their exploits, carved their names into the stone and had statues of themselves erected throughout the sites. They include Ramesses II, Seti I, Tuthmosis III, Hatshepsut and Amenhotep III to name just a few. Amongst Amenhotep III's building work was the Temple of Amun at Luxor, the third pylon at Karnak and of course the Colossi of Memnon at his own mortuary temple. The Hypostyle hall at Karnak was built by Seti I and completed by Ramesses II.

Titles of the king included 'Lord of the Two Lands' (Nb t3wy), 'King of Upper and Lower Egypt' (Nswt- bity) and as previously stated 'Son of Re' (S3 Re). As supreme ruler he would take the country to war should Egypt be threatened, or if he might purely wish to expand his borders, engaging in warfare should the need arise.

Adhering to his duties and honouring the gods, the king would be seen to be upholding the laws of Maat. Should Pharaoh be deemed derelict in his duty, then his reputation was at risk, and his reign and life were put in jeopardy.

To ensure the bloodline was pure, incest was not uncommon amongst royalty, for that reason a brother might marry a sister or half-sister and it has been known for a father to marry a daughter, as this was not deemed a criminal act in pharaonic Egypt. Ramesses II (the Great), sired over 100 children, but it was his 13t^h son Merenptah who succeeded him as Ramesses outlived many of his children, and was approximately ninety years old when he died. The gods obviously looked favourably upon him.

Pharaoh was primarily judge and jury, the state only investigating major crimes, those of regicide, grave robbing, attacks on royalty and defiling the gods. As a king with other duties, and the whole of Egypt to rule, it was necessary to entrust high officials to deal with perpetrators, they would listen to the defendants' pleas, subsequent to the accusations being read out. Should the defendant(s) be found innocent then they would be released, but if found guilty then Pharaoh would be informed and his judgement would be carried out. In the normal course of things, execution was the punishment meted out for crimes against the state.

Unlike today's laws, there were no crime statistics recorded in ancient Egypt, all our information regarding felonies comes through literary evidence and various images. Shards of stone and pottery known as ostraca have been discovered in the workers' village at Deir el-Medina, where the workers have written grocery lists, complaints, and even what their neighbours were up to, such as who was sleeping with whom, fighting and general chit chat, the fore-runner to Face-book.

In Egyptian society no one was above the law, high social status did not secure protection from suspicion or punishment. Pharaoh was seen as a divine king, a living God, an intermediary between the common people and the deities. As such he was responsible for maintaining Maat, failure to do so caused chaos, for instance, failure of the annual inundation. Obviously, we recognize that Pharaoh was not to blame for this problem, which has been solved by the Aswan Dam regulating the Nile's flow, however in antiquity, everything revolved around honouring the deities to avoid disorder and disaster.

As a result of unsuccessful harvests there would be little or nothing to trade or with which to feed the populace. Artisans producing their wares from flax, papyrus and other commodities haggled for necessities as this was a moneyless society until c.300 BC. Apart from the bartering system which was standard, they used a system where metal was weighed into "deben" with one deben being equal to approximately 90g of metal, the amount accrued would be offset against the cost of the goods required. On the occurrences of bad harvests, the resulting prospect of starvation and lack of goods, fuelled some of the people into desperate action causing anarchy.

During the reign of Ramesses III (Dynasty 20), labourers at Deir el-Medina, the workers' village, complained to the officials that they had no food as they had not been paid with their rations of grain, beer, fish etc. These were the men who built the Pharaohs' tombs, and lived with their families near to the necropolis worksite. Their only course of action was to down tools, and this is reported to be the first recorded labour strike in history. The Turin Strike Papyrus, written by the scribe Amennakhte at Deir el-Medina, informs us of the days of the strike and the workmen's complaints.

However, Ramesses' troubles were only beginning, the priests were extremely wealthy and becoming problematic; they would eventually, as High Priests of Amun, rule from Thebes during the Third Intermediate Period, with Smendes I ruling from Tanis as the first Pharaoh of Dynasty

21. On top of this there was discontent within the palace, and a conspiracy was being hatched, which will be discussed later.

AMENHOTEP IV (AKHENATEN)

Pharaoh Amenhotep IV as he was originally known, took it upon himself to initiate the abolition of the standard deities whom Egyptians had worshipped for thousands of years. He changed his name to Akhenaten, associating himself and his family with the Aten -–the sun disc, in order to disassociate himself from Amun/Amen, whose name he ordered to be destroyed wherever it was written. He built a new city known as Akhetaten at Tell el-Amarna (hence the Amarna era), which was abandoned following his demise when the court returned to Thebes. After his death he suffered the awful punishment of '*damnatio memoriae*" which translates as "condemnation of memory" therefore his name was destroyed, and in the Abydos King List his name is omitted. In the hereafter it was essential that something of the person remained for them to have everlasting life, a statue, their name, their body. With the erasure of his name the Egyptians were intending to expunge him from history and eternity. This was obviously not successful.

Akhenaten was not the only one to suffer this fate. Hatshepsut who was standing in as regent for Tuthmosis III (Egypt's "Napoleon") until he became of age, coveted the throne and had herself crowned Pharaoh. Tuthmosis for some reason, did not remove her from authority, perhaps he did not wish to disturb Maat, and at this time he was being well trained in the army. But after her death, her effigies, titles and anything bearing her name were destroyed. She is another who is missing from the 'Kings List" though her mortuary temple at Deir el-Bahri still stands as a testament to her greatness, and as with Akhenaten, both their names have survived despite great efforts to erase them from history.

Illustration 5 - Akhenaten (Author's photograph)

Illustration 6 - Hatshepsut's Temple at Deir el-Bahri
(Author's photograph)

GODS AND GODDESSES

Gods and goddesses were at the forefront of religion, and were all-important in the lives of the ancient Egyptians, whether the person be rich or poor, royal or commoner, therefore an abundance of temples and shrines were constructed in honour of them. Men such as Ptahhotep, Ani and Amenemope all instructed the people to revere their gods, whether at home or in the temples.

One of the largest temples is the Temple of Karnak in Thebes, modern day Luxor, constructed over time by various Pharaohs including Ramesses I, II and III, Seti I, Queen Hatshepsut, Tuthmosis I and others, with the smaller Luxor Temple connected to Karnak via an avenue of sphinxes. The Temple of Isis at Philae and the Temple of Hathor at Dendera are among the most stunning examples of Egyptian architecture. All these temples and others throughout Egypt contained a statue of the god they were dedicated to as opposed to Solar temples which did not contain a statue, as these were dedicated to the sun god Re. They were open to the elements where the sun could shine down into the building.

Many countless deities were portrayed in various anthropomorphic forms such as Horus, who is depicted with the head of a falcon and the body of a human; Anubis is shown with a jackal's head and human body; Thoth with an Ibis head and human body; although they could also be shown in full animal form. Pharaohs were too busy to observe the deities' daily rituals, consequently priests ensured that the duties of washing, feeding, and clothing the divine statues on a daily basis were observed, along with reciting customary prayers.

Throughout Egypt, these iconic buildings portray numerous representations of the deities either carved into the stone or painted on the walls. Some of these deities are often a combination of two or more as in, for example, Amun-Re; both of whom were initially, individual major gods in their own right. Amun moved from being a local Theban god to being head of the pantheon. Re became the most important as the sun God and had more than one title. He was known as Re-Horakhty, Re-Atum and also Re-Horakhty-Atum, the sun in the morning and evening. On joining with Amun, the two became the supreme god of Egypt.

People also worshiped their favourite deity at home, such as Bes the dwarf god who was said to protect children, the home and pregnant women. He was also reputed to be a god of war, and alternatively associated with "humour, music, dancing and sexuality"[1], along with being able to avert evil and ward off bad luck.

There are innumerable gods and goddesses, most of whom at some point merge with other deities, but the ones which will mostly be referred to are: -

Osiris (Wsir/3sir) who was god of the dead and ruler of the underworld. His jealous brother Seth murdered him, and chopped up and distributed Osiris's remains throughout Egypt. Osiris's sister/wife Isis, along with Nephthys, another sister, recovered his body parts, and bandaged them in place. With the assistance of Anubis (Inpw), they brought him back to life, at which point Isis conceived their son Horus. Osiris therefore became the first 'mummy', and presides over the trials in the Hall of Judgement. He grants life to the earth from the underworld by allowing vegetation to grow and the Nile to flow.

Pharaohs associated themselves with Osiris and became one with the god at death. Ramesses II in his temple at Abu Simbel, shows himself as Pharaoh and Osiris at the same time. At Medinet Habu, Ramesses III is shown in Osirian form in his statues.

---

1   Wilkinson, R. H. *The Complete Gods and Goddesses of Ancient Egypt.* Thames and Hudson, London, 2003

Thoth (Djehuty/Ḏḥwty), a moon deity, god of scribes and wisdom. He could be depicted as either a baboon with a moon and crescent moon on his head or as a human with the head of an Ibis. This is the form which is most common and recognisable. The Ibis's beak is long and curved, similar to a writing quill, hence the association with writing. He noted the results of the deceased's heart being weighed against the feather of Maat during the weighing of the heart ceremony in the Hall of Judgement.

Re who was the sun god, later joined with Amun to become Amun-Re, a supreme solar deity. Many Pharaohs associated themselves with this god and gave themselves the title of 's3 rᶜ - *Son of Re'* and he was vital to Egyptian beliefs; travelling the sky during the day, sailing through the underworld at night and being reborn in the morning, the sun god continued the cycle of bringing forth a new day. In picture images Re is swallowed by Nut the sky goddess at night and reborn in the morning after travelling through her body.

Maat goddess of law and order, it is her laws which bring stability as opposed to chaos (Isfet - *isfet*). Maat is identifiable by a feather on her head which is used during the weighing of the heart ceremony, deciding the deceased's honesty and integrity whilst on earth. Pharaohs often have in their cartouches 'beloved of Maat' along with their names, associating themselves with the goddess. In the Hall of Judgement, the council of gods is referred to as the 'Council of Maat'.

Wsir/ Ꜣsỉr 𓊨𓁹

Illustration 7 - Osiris sitting in the Hall of Judgement

(Author's photograph)

Ḏḥwty 𓁟𓆓

Illustration 8 - Thoth

(Author's photograph)

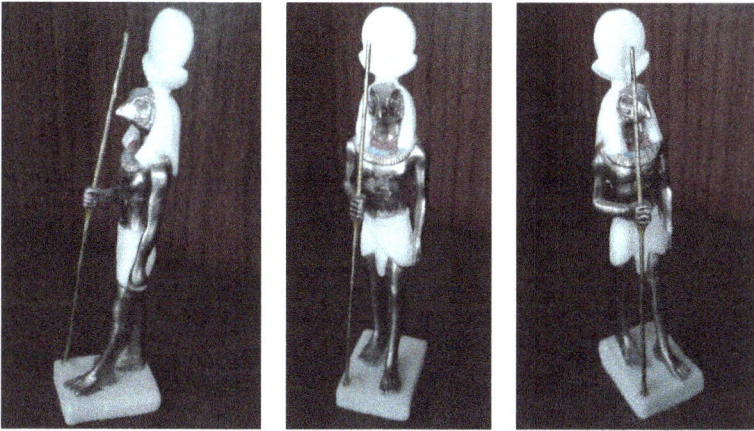

Illustration 9 - Replica of Re the sun God
(Author's statue)

Imn R -Nb pt
Illustration 10 - Amun-Re, Lord of the sky (Heaven)
(Author's photograph)

m3ct

Illustration 11 - Maat
(Author's photograph)

THE LAW OF MAAT

She was the epitome of law and order, everything which was considered faultless, pure, true and moral. Egyptians lived according to her rules, or paid the price.

In the Hall of Judgement, a person's heart was placed on one side of the scales of justice opposite the feather of Maat. This was known as "the Weighing of the Heart Ceremony" If both sides balanced, Thoth recorded the judgement and the deceased would be allowed to enter eternity; should the heart weigh heavy, it was perceived to be bad and Ammit, also known as "the Devourer" was waiting at the side of the scales to eat it. Devouring the deceased's heart caused the deceased to "die the second death" there would be no eternity for them, they became a non-entity, a ghost.

In depictions of the beast and in mythology, the demon animal is referred to as female and she is shown with the head of a crocodile, a lion or leopard's torso and a hippopotamus's hind quarters. In Illustration 13, we see Ammit along with Anubis, Thoth and Osiris, god of the dead, in the Hall of Judgement with the deceased.

Anubis is leading the deceased into the hall and then is kneeling under the scales whilst the heart is being weighed. Thoth is ready with his quill and scroll to record the result and Ammit is waiting for the outcome. The feather of Maat is on the right scale and the heart on the left. On this occasion the balance is even and the deceased subsequently travels on to the afterlife to become one of the blessed dead, 'im3h m3ᶜ ḥrw (the revered one true of voice or the revered or justified).

Illustration 12 - Weighing of the Heart
(Author's photograph)

COMMUNITIES

Towns and villages were close-knit communities where more often than not, secrets were difficult to keep. Consequently, law-breaking could not always be hidden from the eyes and ears of neighbours, therefore it was prudent to aim to 'stay in their good books' and be cautious of what is said to whom. Breaking the law resulted in chaos, disturbing the natural order of things, consequently the perpetrator was brought in for interrogation, and punished accordingly depending upon the severity of the crime.

Higher status individuals decided that even breaking the law in order to provide a little extra was acceptable; how did others in the community survive without resorting to theft? Was it purely a case of greed which prompted the thieves to take their chosen course of action, since according to history, surplus grain from abundant years, was placed in storage for distribution to the populace in lean times. Why, if this was fairly circulated amongst the population, would there be any cause for theft, endangering not only themselves but their families and neighbours?

On the other hand, there is the possibility that at times grain stores were depleted. Under these circumstances many could face starvation, attested to by the famine stela during the reign of Djoser, a famine which lasted seven years. In a later era, Ankhtifi, from the First Intermediate Period, tells us that parents resorted to eating their children during another such food crisis. Whether this is an accurate testimony by Ankhtifi, is debateable, as ancient Egyptian writers and scribes were prone to exaggeration and flowery prose in order to make a point.

Once detained on suspicion of committing a felony, the defendant was taken to 'the place of examination' where torture was often administered to obtain a confession. From time to time other members of the family and acquaintances were also interrogated, they might give up information if they knew anything, in an attempt to save their own skins.

Social contacts, and gang members often under duress, would on occasion give up the names of others involved in a crime, in the hope of a lighter sentence. Some would even go as far as to plant evidence to guarantee a conviction. We will see an example of this in Chapter 4.

MORALITY

Morality in ancient Egypt was all important to the welfare and stability of the people. They lived by the code of Maat, the Goddess of truth, justice and morality.

Moral aspects are to be found in various writings such as *The Instruction of Amenemope*[2] '*The Instruction of Ptahhotep*[3]' and '*The Instruction of* Ani'. There are too many to discuss, therefore below are given a few which are of importance, and which are related in modern day speech.

Firstly, from Ptahhotep: -

- Do not belittle anyone if you are more knowledgeable, there are those wiser than yourself

- Take control of your actions, avoid striking out in anger or frustration either by force or by words

- Leaders are required to uphold the law for justice to prevail, they should not twist the facts

- Do not be greedy, accept what you are given, do not crave more when you are a visitor

- Work hard and increase your wealth, be of good standing in the community

2   Lichtheim, M. *Ancient Egyptian Literature, The New Kingdom.* Vol. II, University of California Press, Berkley and Los Angeles: 1976, 148
3   Lichtheim, M. *Ancient Egyptian Literature, Old and Middle Kingdom.* Vol. I, University of California Press, Berkley and Los Angeles: 1973, 63

- When relating a message given to you, do not add or remove information

- Heed your father's teachings and do not boast

- Respect your betters/elders, family and those you work for, strive to do better

- Do not trespass on another's land, do not steal his property

- Give good advice, be generous and do not lie especially for personal gain

Secondly these are written in '*The Instructions of Ani*[4]' known from the Papyrus Boulaq 4, dating from c.21st/22nd Dynasty. A father is teaching his son the rights and wrongs of life.

- Marry young and have children, it is good to increase your family, a man is regarded for his position in the community, do well and work hard, increase your wealth

- Do not neglect the gods, honour them and give them praise

- Only enter a person's home when invited, do not just walk in

- Do not fornicate with a strange woman

- Do not fight, no good will come of it, god will rebuke the offender(s)

---

4   Lichtheim, M. *Ancient Egyptian Literature, The New Kingdom.* Vol. II, University of California Press, Berkley and Los Angeles: 1976, 135

- Do not get drunk, your mouth may speak evil

- Do not control your wife she knows what she is doing and will run the household efficiently

- Listen and live by your father's words, live a blameless life

With regard to Amenemope[5], his teachings are more relaxed in the respect of how wealthy a person is in order to be able of worth in the community. Not being rich is no longer deemed to be bad luck, a man is now seen as being 'rich' if he is content, works hard, is kind and gentle, has whatever possessions he and his family need and reveres his god(s). There are many more instructions on how one should behave, but these seem to be the most appropriate to maintain stability in a person's life and to avoid conflict and chaos. In essence the basis for a stable community and homelife.

It might be suspected that most parents would be giving this advice to their offspring, but obviously there were those who chose to neglect their teachings, and walked down the wrong path. As Ptahhotep states, 'no-one is perfect', and we all make mistakes, and he relates in his teachings that if a child disobeys his father's words, misbehaves and talks evil then he should be "punished firmly, chastised soundly[6]", in the hope that this will deter the child from wrong-doing. On the other hand, he also says that to punish when no crime has been committed, will turn the "complainer

---

5   Amenemope's instructions can be found in the British Museum Papyrus 10474; portions of it in Stockholm; 3 writing tablets in Turin, Paris, Moscow and an Ostracon in the Cairo Museum. And also in Lichtheim, M. *Ancient Egyptian Literature, The New Kingdom.* Vol. II, University of California Press, Berkley and Los Angeles: 1976, 148

6   Lichtheim, M. *Ancient Egyptian Literature, The Old and Middle Kingdoms.* Vol I, University of California Press, Berkley and Los Angeles: 1973, 73

into an enemy[7]". In other words, if the father chastises his offspring out of temper, when the child has done no wrong, then the father will become his child's enemy, possibly sending him down the wrong road to crime.

Crimes were varied and ranged from lying, and stealing right through to murder, and in another chapter, some crimes will be discussed, along with who the perpetrators were, why they were found guilty, and the punishments meted out to the various culprits where their sentences are known.

Evidence of law and order is found in extant writings, art, fiction, archaeology and in the works of classical authors such as Diodorus Siculus, Manetho and Herodotus, the latter of whom declared *'Egypt is the gift of the Nile'*.

LAW ENFORCEMENT

Diodorus[8] tells us that ten men from each of the following areas of Heliopolis, Thebes and Memphis will be made judges. From these thirty they *"chose the best and elect him Chief Justice and another man from the city stands in his stead[9]."*

Whilst court was in session, the chief justice placed before him the laws which were in a compilation of eight volumes, along with the written statements of those who were appealing for justice. Much like our jury of twelve, the appointed thirty judges decided on a verdict followed by the chief justice placing the 'truth' icon atop the appropriate written petition

---

7   ibid
8   Giles, Laurèn (Edited by). *The Historical Library of Diodorus the Sicilian in Forty Books, Vol 1, Books 1-14:* Sophron Editor, 2014, 53 line 75
9   ibid

presented to him. A gold Maat pendant in the British Museum may have been the legal officials' badge of office, which viziers and chief justices possibly wore.

An example of a complaint which could be taken to the authorities is the Tale of the Eloquent Peasant, whose name is Khun-Anup, very articulate in speech and who seeks the help of the high steward Rensi, after being robbed by Nemtynakht, a man of higher standing.

Khun-Anup was walking along the path with his donkey, when he encountered Nemtynakht, who on seeing the peasant was tempted to take the donkey. He wished he had some type of magic in order to obtain the animal and goods and at this point sent his servant back home to fetch a shawl.

This he laid on the ground from the edge of the water to the edge of his field of barley, consequently barring Khun-Anup's way. Therefore, he took his donkey to higher ground avoiding the shawl. Nemtynakht asked if he was going to use his barley for a road and the peasant said that his way was barred and asked to be allowed to travel along the common path.

Unfortunately, whilst attempting to go on his way, Khun-Anup's donkey ate one 'wisp of barley and Nemtynakht took the animal in recompense. Khun-Anup pleaded for the return of his goods with no success and told Nemtynakht he knew Rensi the high steward and would seek his assistance. At being thus threatened by a lowly peasant, Nemtynakht gave Khun-Anup a beating.

After ten days of pleading and receiving no satisfaction, Khun-Anup, the peasant eventually took his complaint to Rensi.

"O High steward, my lord! .... punish the robber, save the sufferer ....[10]"

Rensi is so thrilled with the peasant's rhetoric that he reports it to Nebkaure the king. Eventually, after nine expressive speeches, the peasant is given justice and compensation.

Although Nemtynakht committed a crime against the peasant and was cruel to him, his deeds may not follow him to the grave. Being of average wealth, he would inevitably be given a good funeral with all the necessities to see him pass through the Hall of Judgement. He would most likely have a heart scarab inscribed with spell 30B from the Book of the Dead to avoid testimony against him, when his heart would be weighed on the scales of justice.

POLICE

The police attempted to ensure order was maintained, that the tombs were safe from robbers and they accompanied higher officials when making arrests. Trained monkeys were often used by the police, similar to our officers on the force today, who use dogs to assist in the prevention of the culprit escaping.

In the tomb of Niankhkhnum and Khnumhotep, a piece of wall art depicts a trained monkey apprehending a thief, by grabbing him by the leg. Here he is caught in the act and as such would have no option but to confess his crime. The criminal would make a statement which started with an oath, *"If I speak falsehood may I be mutilated/exiled..."* which, to all intent and purpose made the punishments harsher. Mutilation was performed on various parts of the body, sometimes to obtain a true confession, as an

---

10   Lichtheim, M. *Ancient Egyptian Literature, The Old and Middle Kingdoms.* Vol. 1. University of California Press: Berkeley and Los Angeles, 1973, 175

extra punishment prior to execution or as the punishment itself, a grisly affair either way. However, should the criminal be in possession of an inscribed heart scarab, and only punished but not executed, then he too may pass through to eternity.

Many must surely have lived in fear when family and neighbours were breaking the law, as everyone was well aware of the consequences. Even if they themselves were not involved in the offence, they could be questioned, and to be aware of a felony and not report it, was a crime in itself.

Civil courts were held for a number of problems ranging from debt, neighbourly disputes against a person or their land, theft, besides many other public difficulties. Punishments for theft incorporated the return of the stolen goods and quite often, twice what was originally stolen plus a fine, whilst minor dispute outcomes were determined between the people involved, and only taken to a magistrate if the problem could not be resolved.

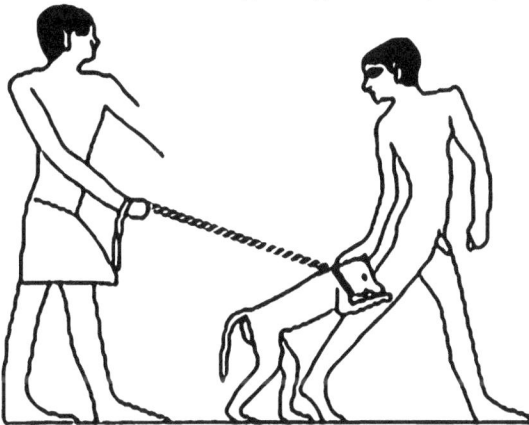

Illustration 13 - Official and monkey apprehending a thief in a tomb
(By courtesy of Dr. Joyce Tyldesley, from her book Daughters of Isis, figure 23)

CHAPTER TWO

Regicide

There were a number of attempts of regicide and of coups in ancient Egypt, some of which were successful, and others which failed. Fortunately, these types of crimes were, in effect, few, commonly committed during times of instability. Those which are known begin with Teti I who ruled during the Old Kingdom, he was the first king of Dynasty 6 c.2345 BC, and culminate with Ramesses III c.1182 BC of Dynasty 20 in the New Kingdom.

According to Manetho, Teti I S3 R^c (son of Re), (𓅮𓏤) was either murdered by his bodyguards, eunuchs[11] or by his supposed successor Userkare. Clayton[12] puts Pepi I as his father's successor, though Tyldesley[13] puts a question mark as to whether Userkare might have reigned between the two, and Dodson and Hilton[14] also name Userkare between Teti and Pepi in the royal succession list of the 6th Dynasty. There is, therefore,

---

11   An Egyptian priest who lived during the 3rd Century BC and wrote the Aegyptiaca (History of Egypt) partly preserved in later sources
12   Clayton, P. A. *Chronicle of the Pharaohs, The Reign by Reign Record of the Rulers and Dynasties of Ancient Egypt.* Thames and Hudson: London 1994, 2006, 64
13   Tyldesley, J. *The Pharaohs.* Quercus Publishing Plc: London 2009,.56
14   Dodson A. and Hilton D. *The Complete Royal Families of Ancient Egypt.* Thames and Hudson: London 2004, 70

contention, as to whether Userkare ruled between the two, and if so, did he murder Teti.

At Saqqara, tombs were discovered during excavations, and these were found to belong to Teti's bodyguards. In one of the tombs a relief was discovered depicting a man without a nose, his feet were amputated and his name had been removed. This is an indication that he had committed some atrocious act, and thus an attempt had been made to prevent him entering eternity, and minus his name along with other parts of his anatomy, he would be unrecognisable and therefore unable to enter the afterlife.

Another mortuary chapel in the area still displayed a name above the door which had obviously been overlooked when everything else had been chiselled out. It states the name of *"Hezi, vizier to king Teti,"* one more member of the gang who allegedly killed the Pharaoh. A Vizier was the second highest authority in the land, he answered only to Pharaoh, and was Pharaoh's right-hand man who held an extremely trusted position within the palace.

The damage on the door surround is obvious, and was caused by removing the images and his name, in order to destroy his ka. Along with Hezi, it is known that the Chief Physician and Overseer of the Armoury both suffered the same *damnatio memoriae* (condemnation of memory). Evidence indicates they too were obviously guilty of a heinous crime, or involved in a conspiracy to commit one.

The family appeared plagued by murderous intent, as the attempted assassination of Meryre Pepi I (𓇳𓄤𓏤𓏤) (𓊪𓊪𓏤𓏤), Teti's' son, was we are told, instigated by one of his queens. In order to discover the truth, Pepi instructed his friend Weni, who held the positions of judge and army commander amongst other titles to hear her trial. It is stated in the

'*Inscription of Weni*[15]' that he was instructed by Pharaoh to enter the royal harem and question the queen alone. We can only assume the queen's fate if she was found guilty and punished, as there are no documents relating to the outcome of the trial. Several academics name and believe the queen, referred to in this text as 'Great of Sceptre"(Weret-Imtes), to have been the instigator. Whoever the guilty party was, we know that Pepi survived, sitting on the throne for a total of approximately fifty years.

Regarding the murder of Sehetepibre Amenemhat I, ⟨○|☥♗⟩ ⟨═🐦⬥⟩ ⟨○|☥♗⟩ ⟨═🐦⬥⟩, Dynasty 12, this is a notable affair due to the information gained from the instructions relayed to his son Senusret I (Sesostris I), who was, at the time, on a campaign in Libya. Amenemhat states that he had finished his supper and went to lie down for an hour's rest. As he was dozing, he became aware of arguing and weapons being wielded. Being half asleep and unprepared without help, Amenemhat was outnumbered and received, what appear to have been, fatal wounds.

"Thus bloodshed occurred while I was without you; before I had sat down with you so as to advise you."[16]

Was this written as the king lay dying, if we consider the script "*bloodshed occurred ... before I had sat down with you*' then it certainly appears that the Pharaoh was probably dying at the point of writing, therefore he could have dictated it to his scribe. Also depending on one's view of the afterlife we have to consider whether it was, in actual fact, his spirit relaying events to the son from the other side, and his son dictated his father's words to his own scribe.

---

15 Lichtheim, M. *Ancient Egyptian Literature, The Old and Middle Kingdoms*. Vol. 1. University of California Press: Berkeley 1973, 19
16 Lichtheim, M. *Ancient Egyptian Literature, The Old and Middle Kingdoms*. Vol. 1. University of California Press: Berkeley 1973, 137

Unfortunately, there appears to be no evidence that the assassins were captured and punished.

The final assassination I shall discuss, is The Harem Conspiracy, which is attested by evidence in the Judicial Papyrus (which is in Turin), and is a section of the Harem Conspiracy Papyrus. This murder for me, is the most memorable, somewhat reminiscent of Henry VIII, in that in order to replace a royal personage on the throne, they resort to killing an innocent party.

The attack was perpetrated against Ramesses III, last of the great Ramesside rulers who reigned during Dynasty 20.

UserMaatRe MeryAmun Ramesses Heqa Iunu

The main conspirator is understood to be Tiye, a lesser wife of Ramesses III, who sought the throne for her son Pentewere. Although he was not the stated heir, Tiye had a desperate desire for him to succeed his father, so much so that there were numerous perpetrators involved in the crime. These included butlers, scribes, army personnel, and other members of the royal household.

Initially it was thought the attempt had failed, though recent examinations of Ramesses' mummy, show that his throat was cut and the murder successful. A body known as 'The Screaming Mummy' and/or 'Unknown Man E', is believed to be Pentewere who was allegedly given the death penalty, and as royalty, was given the choice of suicide for his part in the conspiracy to murder his father. It is suspected that he took poison to end his life, which gave rise to the name of the mummy, due to the facial contortions endured during the death throes. He is as Elliot Smith tells us, *'without genitalia and is lacking an embalming incision[17]'*.

This body was not mummified in the usual way, was this extra punishment for his crime?

As with Pentewere, some were ordered to take their own lives, some were executed and others were punished by the removal of noses and ears. The various punishments were meted out as the law demanded.

Ramesses' murder was a fruitless endeavour on which the royal wife and son embarked, as his chosen successor Ramesses IV would also have needed to be murdered, in order to gain the throne. As it turned out, although the assassination attempt succeeded, Ramesses IV did indeed follow his father as ruler of Egypt.

---

17   Smith, G. E. *The Royal Mummies.* Imprimerie de l'Institut Français d'Archéologie Orientale: Cairo 1912., Reprinted Gerald Duckworth & Co. Ltd: London 2000, 115

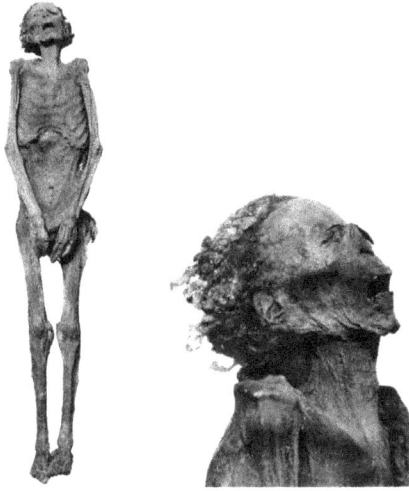

Illustrations 14 - Unknown Man E (aka - The Screaming Mummy/Pentewere)
(From G. Elliot Smith, The Royal Mummies, 1912, plate XCIV and plate XCV)

There are also undocumented crimes, such as that of the naturally formed mummy 'Gebelein Man' c.3500BC, discovered c.1896 and nicknamed 'Ginger' because of his hair colour. His interment directly into the sand has ensured his corpse is well preserved, and this has enabled scientists to ascertain his demise. Using modern technology, they have exposed a wound determining that he was stabbed in the back. Was it murder or execution? His age is dated between 18-21years old with a muscular physique. Ginger is one of the oldest mummies discovered to date and is housed in the British Museum. Scientists have constructed a 'virtual autopsy table' which visitors can use to learn about this man. Whether or not his attackers were found and punished is unknown.

If Gebelein man was murdered and placed into a grave, who put everyday items in with him, and why? Surely a murderer would not do so. Was his body discovered by family and or friends? Did they give him a decent burial, but why was he naked?

There are questions to be answered regarding Ginger, but let us hope his god(s) looked favourably on him.

CHAPTER THREE

Grave Robbing

Ancient Egyptians were not obsessed with death, they were preoccupied with survival in the afterlife, and preparing themselves and ensuring their affairs were in order for them to spend eternity in the "field of reeds" - their concept of heaven. Therefore, what they owned in life they took with them to the grave to be used in the hereafter.

It was not only the Pharaoh who enjoyed such pleasures, the governors, scribes, elite and skilled craftsmen from Deir el-Medina were also hoping for an eternal existence. In the private tombs, excavations have revealed wooden models of cattle, breweries, bakeries, soldiers, games and scenes of everyday life.

The poorer population took with them their meagre belongings, also hopeful for life ever after. Unable to afford grand burials, their bodies would have been wrapped in a cloth and most likely buried directly into the sand in the desert, or in the necropolis. It has been noted that children were often buried under the floors in houses, attested by Flinders Petrie who discovered infants buried below houses during his excavations.

Where the rich were concerned, mortuary formulae such as the Pyramid Texts, Coffin Texts and the Book of the Dead were painted on the tomb walls, coffins and coffin lids to assist the deceased to enter the afterlife. The elite or pharaonic coffin was usually made from wood, and encased inside a larger wood or stone coffin which would then be placed inside the sarcophagus, normally carved from stone. Along with mummification, the multiple coffins assisted in the preservation of the body; we can see this in the various mummies on display in museums. One would think this made it more difficult for the robbers to gain access; but unfortunately, this was not always the case. Very few tombs avoided desecration.

Pharaohs and the elite were prime targets for robbery and therefore every effort was made to make their final resting places as secure as possible. During the Old and Middle Kingdoms, the pharaohs chose to be buried in pyramids, and by the New Kingdom were constructing their tombs in the Valley of the Kings.

However, 'where there is a will there is a way" and thieves managed to achieve entry, breaking into pyramids at Saqqara, Abydos, Hawara and tombs in the Valley of the Kings, Valley of the Queens and other areas. As far as the tomb raider was concerned, everything in the tomb was just waiting to be taken, the owner was not using it, why should they not benefit from selling some items. Many of the smaller items such as jewellery, statuettes, daggers etc., were easy to remove, and the proceeds gained from the sale would ensure a better lifestyle. Tomb robbing in general was a lucrative affair, if the perpetrators were not caught, and it was not just the poor who stole, even the upper classes were often involved.

There are texts which tell of crime, such as the "Admonitions of Ipuwer" from the Middle Kingdom:- *"The land is full of gangs. Crime is everywhere... the robber. The servant takes what he finds... hearts are violent. The noble is a thief...*[18] "

---

18 Lichtheim, M, *Ancient Egyptian Literature*, The Old and Middle Kingdoms, Vol. 1., University of California Press; Berkley 1973, 150-151

The text goes on to say how death is everywhere, people are buried in the river, even the embalmer's secrets are discarded and nothing is as it was. Chaos was everywhere and the people took what they wanted from each other, palaces and tombs.

Tombs were sacred places, especially those of the Pharaohs who were now, in death, deemed to be gods, specifically Osiris, and as such passed on their powers to their son, and/or the next pharaoh In an attempt to avoid the pillaging of royal tombs, huge stone doors were installed at the entrance; tunnels and shafts were incorporated into the design and enormous blocks of granite or stone secured corridors and chambers, especially the burial chamber, the robbers' ultimate goal.

Usually, once the pharaoh's tomb was closed, a seal was placed on the exterior door, as was the case with Tutankhamun. This seal was depicted with a jackal and nine prisoners (the nine bows), their arms tied behind their backs and a rope around each of their necks keeping them altogether. Along with the seal, there was a thick, heavy rope attached to the seal and the opposite door handle. This outer door seal was not originally intact at the time of Howard Carter's discovery, as it had been resealed later after an attempted robbery, but within the tomb other seals were undisturbed.

In the event of someone gaining entry, there was the chance that they might fall foul of some dreadful fate, as some believed from a curse which had been placed upon the tomb or they might plunge into a concealed trap. Often curses were inscribed on the entrances, though these did not deter the thieves, possibly due to the fact that the scribes were the ones mainly able to decipher the writings. Not many ancient Egyptians learned to read or write, only the lucky few from the whole population.

Their belief in curses dwindled, as time after time they entered the burial places without being struck down, so obviously the gods were oblivious to their escapades. In the Manchester University Museum, there is an artefact discovered during the excavation of a tomb. It is known as the "Riqqeh Pectoral", named after the area in which it was discovered and when found was in the skeletal hand of an ancient tomb robber. It appears that the thief was crushed in the tomb by falling debris, so maybe there is something in the curse after all.

Another hopeful deterrent was the 'magic bricks', the oldest being found not in a royal tomb, but that of Amenemhat (Theban Tomb 82). He was a high dignitary, his position being steward to the vizier, and the vizier was second to the Pharaoh. These special bricks were made to a specified construction, as detailed from the text written on them in hieroglyphs or hieratic; the writings stated in which direction each one had to be set into the niches. The role the bricks played were to protect the deceased from dangers in all directions, as they were placed according to the four cardinal points of the compass.

Within the construction of the brick was an indentation in which an amulet was placed. The West brick held the Djed pillar, East was for Anubis, South the flame and North contained the figure of a mummy on a pedestal. These bricks of protection are inscribed with a text from the Book of the Dead, chapter 151[19]. Texts on the magic bricks contain warnings such as this one in the tomb of Amenemhat "... *[I] will not allow you to hinder me, ... I will not allow you to attack, I will attack you ... I will protect Osiris, the scribe Amenemhat ...*"[20]. Is this another source from which the curse of the tombs comes?

The act of grave robbing was a heinous crime, but to defile the human remains was the ultimate sacrilege. Robbing a sealed tomb was not an easy task, it was far harder and riskier than stealing from a tomb currently

---

19   Gahlin, Lucia, *Egypt, Gods, Myths and Religion*, Lorenz Books, an imprint of Anness Publishing Ltd, London, 2001, 2007, 157.

20   https://osirisnet.net/tombes/nobles/amenemhat82/e_amenemhat82_06.htm

under construction. During building small items could easily be hidden beneath clothes, though one must be careful to avoid being seen, the consequences would be dreadful for the perpetrator.

How did the robbers pick which tomb to rob? Did they lie and say they were working away and chose a site in another district, or did they opt for one nearer to home? It was not a simple case of entering the building, there was much to consider. Many months of planning were involved including area surveillance, carefully choosing gang members who would hopefully not betray their comrades, deciding on the right time to strike, and offering bribes to corrupt guards or police who would turn a blind eye as long as there was something in it for them.

The tunnelling required specialist workers to carry out the job, including a stonemason and engineer, as described on National Geographic's documentary, "The Egyptian Job" relating to the robbery of Amenemhat III's pyramid.

Hundreds of tons of earth were dug from under the tomb, which they somehow had to dispose of and massive blocks of granite, which sealed various areas, needed to be moved to gain entry. It should be borne in mind that all of this was undertaken using basic tools, in virtual darkness, and that all the robbers had for lighting were oil lamps. There was no electric lighting nor power tools to make it easier for them in antiquity.

With many obstacles to overcome, it is incredible that they managed to reach the burial chamber, never mind gain access. How had they managed to avoid traps and dead ends? Once pharaoh passed over to the 'other side', the belief was that he ensured goodwill and prosperity to his subjects back on earth. Therefore, it was vital he remained undisturbed along with his worldly goods. Unless working on a tomb, preparing it for the future occupant, carrying out a robbery was not completed in a day.

Even then it was a risky business as workers were checked going in and out of the tomb.

Robbers faced the same dangers as our coal miners, that of cave-ins. Where were the excavated earth and rocks disposed of? Taking these outside would attract attention from necropolis guards, leaving them in the tunnel would block an escape route. Where was all the rubbish dumped?

The thieves were led to dead ends, although through a trap door in the ceiling, then through another and by making a hole in the wall, they managed to crawl through into the burial chamber. One of the ways to break quartzite in a tomb is to wet the stone then heat it with a flame and hit it with a hard rock. This causes the quartzite/stone to crack. Repeating this over and over again makes a hole large enough for a person to crawl through.

These thieves were not content just to rob Amenemhat, they committed the most ultimate sacrilege by burning his body to gain access to the amulets and jewellery wrapped within the bandages.

They needed to work fast, obtain the booty and get out with the ill-gotten gains, without detection, and to dispose of the goods on the black market. It was Flinders Petrie who discovered that the burial chamber had been ransacked, when he entered it in 1888[21]. Amenemhat was the last Pharaoh to be buried in a pyramid, and it is believed none of his treasure was recovered and the culprits were, luckily for them, never caught. If one can be permitted to say a heist is ingenious, then this one stands alongside some modern-day robberies.

---

21   Clayton, Peter A, *Chronicle of the Pharaohs, The Reign by Reign Record of the Rulers and Dynasties of Ancient Egypt,* Thames and Hudson; London, 1994, 2006, 88.

Poorer graves were also desecrated for their meagre possessions. Elite burials mainly have robbery attempts at interment, relinquishing the need to return to the tomb. These were most probably committed by those bandaging the bodies (priests), the burial party and even the cemetery guards.

This was a dangerous business and many paid the highest price as did Amenpanufer, a grave robber who escaped punishment on his first capture by bribery, but was not so fortunate when seized a second time.

Illustration 15 - Replicas of two inner anthropoid coffins
(Author's photograph)

CHAPTER FOUR

Amenpanufer – A Tomb Robber

On his accession to the throne, a Pharaoh would choose his eternal resting place, and work would commence, subject to finalisation of the architect's plans. The Theban necropolis on the west bank, famously known as The Valley of the Kings, is where many Pharaohs chose to be buried in the New Kingdom, in order to, with any luck, avoid discovery and desecration. The tombs were hewn deep into the mountain, the chambers and many passages blocked by massive granite slabs, dropped into place as they were being sealed up, as was anticipated, for eternity.

Amenpanufer[22] was a man of twenty years old, middle-aged in ancient Egyptian terms, considering life expectancy was in the region of 40 years. He was, already, a seasoned tomb robber, husband to an eighteen-year-old wife and father to three young children with another on the way.

Amenpanufer was an unskilled quarry labourer, cutting stone for the mortuary temples; however, unlike the skilled workers who lived at Deir el-Medina in what could be called 'moderate luxury', his home of mud-brick was in the poorer district of town. In this small house he lived with

---

22 Gill, Anton, *Ancient Egyptians. The Kingdom of the Pharaohs Brought to Life;* HarperCollins *Entertainment*, an imprint of HarperCollins *Publishers*, London, 2003, 2004, 161-177.

his young family along with his mother. Infant mortality was quite high in those days along with death during childbirth for the mother. His wife was fortunate that up to this point, all her children had been delivered safely, no doubt with the help of the dwarf god Bes who was protector of childbirth and the home amongst his other attributes.

Following his previous arrest for robbing the tomb of Pharaoh Sobekemsaf II, and acquittal after bribing the scribe Khapmope, Amenpanufer continued taking risks, and was now part of another gang of thieves.

Unfortunately, this venture was to take a totally different course.

Taking his chances with this grave robbing gang, he brought home toys for his children, small amulets and goddess statuettes. Being small items, they could hopefully be carried under clothing without detection, and were fairly easy to dispose of if one knew who to trust. At home, he wrapped and placed the goods to be sold in a hidden niche. Next day he took them to Bakwerel, a buyer of illicit goods, who was also the chief of the police, therefore Amenpanufer presumed he was safe.

Who would suspect an officer of the law of handling and accepting stolen goods?

Tomb workers were supervised by the police, and the scribes who recorded which tools were used by the various workmen. These tools were not owned by the labourers, but by the state, and they were logged in and out at the beginning and end of shifts.

Harshire was an honest scribe who worked at Ramesses IX's tomb under Paser, the senior mayor of Thebes and also Pawero, mayor of the west bank. Harshire was a man who kept his eyes and ears open and he now suspected dodgy dealings between the head painter of the tomb Pentaweret, and Userkhepesh the crew's captain. He noticed Pawero and a couple of police talking to the two workmen, then he noticed a small bag being passed from Userkhepesh to Pawero, who put the object inside his clothing, and he did not miss the fact that the police were looking away.

Pentaweret and Userkhepesh began a conversation when they met on their way home, though unbeknown to them, they had been observed by Harshire. He was unsure of their discourse, but was suspicious of the two men.

Pentaweret was accustomed to smuggling, and in the comfort of his house in the village of Deir el-Medina, he removed a golden pectoral. This had been strapped to his chest, which the police on security had failed to notice - or had they? There is the possibility that they were in on the robberies.

Pentaweret's eight-year-old son was aware of his father's dealings and was trusted to keep quiet. Shortly afterwards, Userkhepesh arrived at Pentaweret's house with a full sack, and after checking the stolen items, they wrapped them individually before placing the goods into two donkey panniers. Pentaweret and his son passed the panniers to an accomplice via the roof top, then the group took their booty to the village wall, where a man and donkey were waiting.

Harshire and two other men witnessed the whole event, and, deciding he had enough proof, Harshire chose to report this knowledge to Paser, rather than to Pawero.

Paser listened to Harshire, and secretly deployed some of his men to the west bank to investigate. Unfortunately, Pawero had spies too, and on discovering Harshire's report, needed to act quickly to divert suspicion from himself, as he realised, he was as yet, an unnamed suspect. Advising Bakwerel of the problem they decided that someone in high authority, though not particularly honest, was required to help them escape the investigation; they chose the vizier Khaemwese. Bakwerel also knew of Amenpanufer's previous lucky escape, here was the perfect person to take the blame.

At this point we see corruption at its highest level, as Bakwerel, accompanied by a few of his officers, entered Amenpanufer's home and arrested the young man, whilst the remaining police searched the property. To ensure conviction, Bakwerel brought his own stolen goods to be discovered in the house. Were these the amulets and other items which Amenpanufer had previously sold to him? It would certainly be one way of disposing of them in the current situation, and should Amenpanufer talk, there would be no proof of Bakwerel's guilt to be found in his own quarters.

Khaemwese interrogated Amenpanufer who suffered torture for a few days before he confessed to the crime. Another proof of guilt was to show where the crime had been committed, therefore Amenpanufer and the court travelled to the tomb as the law dictated. To save himself, Pawero showed Khaemwese various tombs in the Valley of the Kings which were intact, satisfying the vizier that there were no surreptitious dealings on this site.

In the meantime, Paser had written to Pharaoh Ramesses IX to instigate an independent investigation, and on hearing this via his own secret agents, Pawero was angry. Subsequently, he informed Khaemwese that there was no truth in the allegations, which, unfortunately for him, were now out in the open.

In the Temple of Karnak, the trial of Amenpanufer and the other robbers was underway. Having been brutally tortured, he had given up his partners in crime, a total of eight thieves, who also under coercion, confessed their offences.

Every word was recorded by the court scribes, as well as the accusations being read out by the Royal Scribe. When it was time for Amenpanufer to speak, he began with the standard oath, *"If I speak falsehood, may I be mutilated [in the nose and ears] and be sent into exile to the Land of Kush"*[23] Considering the fact he had been tortured and more than likely mutilated anyway, this appears to be a futile oath. He then publicly named his accomplices and described in full detail their journey to the tomb of Sobekemsaf, the robbing of it, their desecration of the Pharaoh as they removed him from his sarcophagus, the burning of the coffin to retrieve the gold leaf and the return home with their ill-gotten gains. So, not only was he in trouble for the goods which he stole from Ramesses' tomb, but also with regard to his previous offence.

However, there was more to come as Amenpanufer named the officials he had bribed earlier. This regrettably did not save him or his accomplices, they were all bound and taken to the site of execution. He and his comrades were to face the worst punishment possible; they were to be impaled on a stake via the back passage. Once the executioners lifted them into place and released their hold gravity took over.

They were left at the execution site to decompose, their kas were unable to move away from the place of death, and they would become fodder for the birds and wild animals, no body left for the spirit to recognise in the afterlife. Amenpanufer's afterlife would involve him wandering as a ghostly spirit, enduring many awful punishments throughout eternity. It has been stated that these damned souls were made to walk on their heads and eat their own excrement, their bodies rotted, or were continually burned and beaten, they were to reside in the Egyptian concept of hell.

---

23   Gill, A, *Ancient Egyptians. The Kingdom of the Pharaohs Brought to Life*; HarperCollins *Entertainment*. An imprint of HarperCollins *Publishers*, London 2003, 2004, 171.

In the religious beliefs pharaoh in death was a god, and heinous crimes against a dead pharaoh could bring untold chaos to the land of Egypt, therefore punishments were the most horrendous which could be meted out to the offenders.

Following the executions, an investigation was instigated as robberies continued, and a year later Pentaweret, Userkhepesh, their accomplices and families were apprehended. The ringleaders were executed by impalement and searches including the houses of the elite brought forth many stolen artefacts purchased on the black market.

The scribal accounts of various state crimes have survived in some cases, though not fully. In the Papyrus Leopold II and Amherst, there is written evidence of Amenpanufer's guilt which ultimately sealed his fate and that of his accomplices. It states that once inside the burial chamber they opened the sarcophagus and the coffins, removed the gold, amulets and jewels then set fire to the coffins.

Illustration 16 - Hypostyle Hall at Karnak
(Author's photograph)

Illustration 17 - Hieroglyph for impalement
(Author's drawing)

OTHER CRIMES

At Deir el-Medina, the workmen's village, there was also criminal activity.

Paneb of Dynasty 19 was an orphan, and had been taken in and raised by the chief workman Neferhotep, who passed this position on to his adopted son. Neferhotep's brother Amennakht, was angered by Paneb becoming chief workman when Neferhotep died, as he was expecting to step into his brother's shoes. Amennakht condemns Paneb in the Papyrus Salt 124, suggesting that the post was gained by bribery, and a list of Paneb's supposed misconduct is told in this account. Amongst his alleged misdemeanours were adultery, drunkenness, tomb robbery, and even rape. Was his adoptive uncle telling the truth, or was he being vindictive because Paneb became chief workman?

In the Valley of the Kings Paneb is supposed to have violated Seti Merenptah II's tomb by sitting on the sarcophagus, stripping a chariot, and in another tomb, he stole stone to be cut and used for the pillars in his own. He also took copper chisels from the work place.

Over in the Valley of the Queens, he apparently entered Princess Henutmire's tomb. She was a daughter of Ramesses II, and from here, he stole a mummified goose, though what he would do with this, one is at a loss to imagine. He also entered the tomb of Nakhtmin a worker and stole various funerary objects from here too.

It is obvious, should these accusations have been true, that Paneb did not respect the property of others, and if he had been caught, he would have been lucky to avoid punishment at the highest level.

So, what happened to Paneb? Was he executed, mutilated, condemned into forced labour or banished? After the accusations, his disappearance becomes an enigma, as there is no written evidence from that point onwards.

There are other papyri telling of tomb robberies and these include the Abbot Papyrus number 10221, held in the British Museum, which concerns inspections of tombs in the time of Paser and Pawero. The Papyrus Mayer A states a case where five people were accused, found innocent and released, whilst Papyrus Mayer B deals with the robbery of Ramesses VI's tomb, though the beginning and end of the text are missing.

The Westcar Papyrus mentions burning as a punishment. A tale of 'The Wax Crocodile' is related by Prince Khafre to his father Pharaoh Khufu. This tale ends with a scribe's wife 'tied to a stake and burned to death; her ashes thrown into the Nile.'

Although suspects were taken in on suspicion of guilt, Pharaoh instructed his officers to be certain that a crime had been committed by the accused, before punishment was delivered, and they were warned not to be hasty in their condemnation as is attested in the Judicial Turin Papyrus.

CHAPTER FIVE

Penalties

C rimes which were committed by the general public, and to the general public, were settled within the community, and these offences were dealt with by a town's council of elders. These included attacks on the person such as assault, rape, theft, fights and even murder. Breaches of contract were also sorted out, and, on occasion, divine intervention was used in the form of oracles.

Both the defendant and the plaintiff would have an ostracon placed at either side of the street and, following the hearing, the image of the god, which was held high by the priests, would incline towards whichever decision was deemed appropriate. Once the verdict was given it was accepted as valid, and the guilty party would be treated appropriately.

Obviously, we know that it was the priests making the decision and moving the deity as they saw fit. But, in antiquity where complete belief and trust in the gods were the norm, oracles and their decisions were totally acceptable. This may appear to be an odd form of judgement to us, but the ancient Egyptians believed the gods were benevolent when dedication and proper respect were given to them.

Law enforcement officers were authorised to mete out punishments, but normally, only Pharaoh ordered the death penalty. Should the court deem execution a fitting sentence, the Pharaoh would be informed and his decision would be final. The following punishments have been noted throughout Egyptian history;

- Whipping or beating with a stick, was not only used as a punishment, but also as a death sentence. It has been reported that 100-200 lashes could be imposed along with five cuts.

- In the cases where bastinado was used as chastisement, the soles of the feet were beaten with a cane, which rendered the person barely able to stand, never mind capable of walking.

- Exile, which could include the whole family, and not merely the convicted. This was a dreadful punishment for the family, as no Egyptian wanted to die outside of their country, as there would be no suitable burial for them.

- Imprisonment, though this would be for a minimum time until a suitable punishment was determined. Deserters from the army or the government corvees were sent to jail.

- Mutilation, which included branding, removal of the nose or ear/s, hands, feet and tongue, used as a punishment, but also administered during torture.

- The ultimate penalty was execution, which, depending on the status of the individual, varied enormously. Burning, beheading and impalement have all been recorded, though for a member of the royal household, death by suicide was an option. How to terminate their own life would be of their own choosing, though poison, it seems, was the preferred method.

As previously stated, the Judicial Turin Papyrus lists the names of the perpetrators, their crimes, the trial, and the verdicts, which were given out to each individual accused of conspiring against Ramesses III. The text states how noses and ears were cut off, how the *'great criminal Pebes, former butler'* was sentenced to take his own life, as was Pentewere, the aforementioned screaming mummy. An autopsy has confirmed Pentewere died by poison, due to the contracted shape of his stomach cavity, and modern scans and forensics have confirmed that his body was eviscerated.

He was found in 1886, whilst the head of the Egyptian Antiquities Service, Gaston Maspero, was unwrapping bodies. These had previously been discovered in a royal cache, situated in the Deir el-Bahri valley, near the Valley of the Kings. Amongst the mummies were the famous Pharaohs Ramesses II - (the Great), Seti I, Seqenenre Tao and Tuthmosis III. Therefore, Pentewere must have been someone of very high rank, to be in the presence of these great monarchs.

There were over fifty mummies and thousands of artefacts discovered here by the el-Rassul brothers, who sold on the black-market numerous artefacts, which they had removed from the cache over a period of time.

Pentewere was discovered in an unmarked coffin, and was wrapped in sheep or goatskin, a sign that he had done something dreadful. The marks where his hands and feet were tied were visible, though an attempt had been made to perform some mummification on the body. Furthermore, his burial was quite unusual, because, on the one hand he was being condemned to eternal damnation, and on the other, there was the possibility that someone was trying to give him some sort of peace in the afterlife. This was not standard practice, by Egyptian law he was either damned or not.

But which poison killed him?

The two most common available poisons, were opium and mandrake. As with most poisons, in regulated dosage they assist in effecting pain relief, facilitate sleep for insomnia cases and cleanse wounds, amongst other things. The Egyptians believed mandrake was an aphrodisiac, assisted in conception and when "mixed with water or beer" could induce sleep[24]; and as beer was drunk daily in Ancient Egypt, taken in a large dose, this could have been the poison used to commit suicide.

Alternatively, opium can be prepared into various other drugs including, morphine, heroin and codeine. Ancient Egyptian doctors had excellent knowledge of various plants and herbs, and as they were capable of extracting morphine, I believe they had the knowledge to make a concoction which could be used for inducing death. In the tomb of Kha, a royal architect, and his wife Meryt at Deir el-Medina (Theban Tomb 8 – TT8), a stone vessel was discovered containing morphine attesting to its usage. Was this morphine used for medicinal purposes?

It has been stated that some of those who were executed, suffered death by burning, and this could relate to the women of the harem, and those who knew and failed to report the conspiracy to the authorities.

The Rollin and Lee Papyri also tell of magic, including the use of wax effigies being used, in order to disable the guards, enabling Ramesses' chambers to be entered and the Pharaoh murdered. Could the *Boswellia Sacra* tree - (frankincense), known to be used in magical spells, and also medicine, have been utilised in the effigies?

There is still debate as to whether Ramesses died whilst being attacked or whether he died due to his injuries during the trial; though a cut on his throat which has recently been discovered is believed to be the cause of his demise.

---

24 http://www.thewisemag.com/mystery/the-magic-of-mandrake

PENALTIES: NON-ROYALS AND LOWER-CLASS CITIZENS

Once such people were tried and convicted, any of the above punishments could be handed out. The worst, and one would imagine the most feared, was impalement. There were, it appears two forms of this execution used not only in ancient Egypt but also in other countries, the most famous being imposed by Shaka Zulu, leader of the Zulu tribe of Africa (c.1816AD), and by Vlad the 'Impaler' (c.1456-1477AD), from Wallachia, in what is now modern Romania.

Papyrus Boulaq 18, which is dated to the time of Sobekhotep II, who reigned during Dynasty 13 (c.1750BC), states that "... *the comrade was put on the stake*".

The Abydos Decree of Seti I (c.1290BC Dynasty 19,) at Nauri year 4 states, "*The laws shall be executed against him, by condemning him impaled on the stake ...*".

In the first type of impalement, the convicted was held either face down or face up, above a wooden pole, secured into the ground. The top of the stake was previously spiked or slightly rounded to inflict maximum pain and a slow death.

The second type was as we have seen, via the anus, the punishment dealt to the grave robbers in the previous chapter.

The Narmer Palette depicts Pharaoh in the smiting pose, the prisoner being held by the hair, and Narmer ready to deliver the death blow. On the opposite side of the palette, defeated enemies have been decapitated, therefore beheading was not only used for criminals, but also against captured warriors.

Illustration 18 - Narmer Palette
Author's own artefact
The Narmer Palette showing on the recto Pharaoh slaying a prisoner.

King Narmer many Egyptologists believe is the unifier of ancient Egypt, bringing in the 1st Dynasty of a now united country.

The king wears the White Crown of Upper Egypt on this the reverse side and the Red Crown of Lower Egypt on the verso. This signifies he has defeated Lower Egypt in battle and is now ruler of the whole country.

As became the norm in Egyptian art, artists drew their pictures in registers, showing each part of the story in easy to understand sections. Pharaoh is always shown towering above everyone else, and here, on the recto side of the palette, he is depicted about to execute an Asiatic prisoner. Two already fallen prisoners are shown in the lowest register.

Now, having defeated his enemies, he instructs his artisans to make this palette in commemoration of his victory. With this palette, Narmer, it could be said, sets the scene for future kings who would go on to build far larger monuments depicting their greatness in places such as Karnak and Luxor Temples.

Diodorus Siculus also tells us that although Pharaoh was the highest law in the land, ensuring Maat was upheld, he was also required to maintain his standards within the confines of the judicial system. As he demanded his subordinates to judge justly, it was necessary for him to do the same, dealing out punishment devoid of anger or malice.

There are other crimes for which Diodorus Siculus states the death penalty was mandatory;[25]

- Perjury was amongst these, as to bear false witness under oath was defying the gods.

- Ignoring an attack on another person, or failing to assist them, should one be able to do so, also merited the death penalty.

- If the witness of an attack was unable to help, then they were required to inform the authorities as soon as possible, for failure to do so resulted in the bystander being beaten and they were denied food and water for three days.

- Information regarding occupation was required to be formally written and handed over to the magistrates, and should this not be done, or if false information was given, this too resulted in execution, one finds this penalty bizarre to say the least.

---

25 Edited by Giles, Laurèn, The Historical Library of Diodorus the Sicilian in Forty Books, Vol 1, Books 1-14, Sophron Editor, 2014, Book 1, 48-57

- Although disclosing military secrets was an act against the state, the perpetrators were not executed, as an alternative punishment they had their tongues cut out, and those who falsified written documents, had both their hands cut off.

- In cases where a man touched a married woman, there were two punishments. If he touched her without her consent, then he was emasculated, but if she consented to his advances, he was beaten one thousand times with a rod, and she would have her nose cut off. However, what we do have to remember though, is that there was no formal marriage ceremony between couples, they simply moved in together, and if the relationship was good then they were considered to be in a marriage.

Considering the beliefs of the Egyptians that the body was required to be intact to enter the afterlife, these punishments appear rather harsh.

CHAPTER SIX

Preparing for the Afterlife

Ancient Egyptians believed there were five parts which made up a deceased person's identity.

The heart (*ib* 🝙), as we know, was used at the weighing of the heart, in the Hall of Judgement. It was believed the heart held many secrets, and it was vital in determining whether the deceased was considered pure to continue their journey to eternal life in the 'Field of Reeds'.

The shadow (*šwt* 🧍) was depicted as a small human which was painted black. It was capable of moving around and devouring funerary offerings without the aid of the body. Being free from restrictions to the tomb, and able to wander abroad, the shadow was sometimes shown being accompanied by the Ba bird. We have information regarding this from the tomb of Iri Nufer at Thebes (TT290), where inscriptions and pictures of the Ba and Shadow are depicted. Iri Nufer was a 'servant in the place of truth' (sḏm ꜥš m st m3ꜥt) during the reign of Ramesses II, Dynasty 19, and his title refers to a person who worked in the Theban necropolis, which is situated on the West bank of the Nile.

Illustration 19 - The deceased's
Ba hovering over the mummy
(Author's drawings)

Illustration 20 - Ba Birds
(Author's drawing)

The name (*ren* ◯〰), as previously noted, was of prime importance for survival. A deceased's name would be inscribed on the exterior of his or her tomb, on stela, coffins and on any surface where it could be read. Thus, anyone passing the tomb and reading out the name, would enable the deceased to have eternal existence. This was another reason for the decoration of the tomb; should there be a lull in family and friends leaving sustenance for the deceased, due to the magic in the paintings, nourishment would be permanently available.

The Ba (*b3* 🦅 *or* 🦅), often translated as the soul, was associated with personality and could perform all the physical attributes of the living person, therefore this entity could eat, drink, speak and move. In iconography the *ba* was depicted as a bird, or as a bird with a human head, and sometimes arms, this enabled the dead to leave and return to the tomb. Whilst out of the tomb, the *ba* was capable of self-sufficiency, but it was obligated to return to the tomb at night. In the Book of the Dead, spell 89 allowed the *ba* and the dead body to be re-united *may you cause my ba to come to me from wherever it may be... O heavenly ones, do not appropriate my ba...*".

The Ka (*k3* ⊔), frequently considered as the life force, was referred to as a person's double and was breathed into the baby, by Khnum, who was believed to be the creator of the body which he made on his potter's wheel. He then put the baby into the woman who at the required time, gave birth to the child. As we require sustenance in life, so did the *ka* in the afterlife, a frequent inscription used in funerary texts is, *"for the ka of* (n k3 n ⊔)." Therefore, relatives of the deceased left food and drink in the tomb chapel, next to the false door, from where the ka would emerge, and indulge itself on the sustenance offered, in order to survive. Eventually, if the correct funerary rites were performed and continual offerings were made to the deceased, then the Ba and the Ka united to make the Akh (*3ḫ* 𓅜), a glorified spirit and purportedly a living entity. This Akh could, under the right situations, harm, frighten or even assist the living, again another form of what we would term 'a ghost', either malevolent or benevolent.

All these components are important for the person to attain eternal life.

Illustration 21 - Khnum, a creator god
(Author's statue)

MUMMIFICATION

Egyptian tradition required the body to be intact, properly mummified and interred, in order for the person to enter eternity, ensuring there was a body in which the five supernatural entities could survive. We are aware of three forms of mummification, as related by Diodorus Siculus and Herodotus.

The first was for the upper echelons of society where the brain was removed (excerebration), usually via the nose or alternatively via a hole in the nape of the neck. The internal organs (evisceration) were removed through a cut made on the left side of the abdomen, desiccated for preservation and stored in Canopic Jars. Each jar had a specific purpose: -

Jackal Headed Duamutef protected the stomach and was in turn protected by Neith, Goddess of the East.

Falcon Headed Qebehsenuef was protector of the intestines and he was protected by Serket (or Selket), Goddess of the West.

Baboon Headed Hapi looked after the lungs and his protector was the Northern Goddess Nephthys.

Lastly, Human Headed Imsety was responsible for the liver and was protected by Isis, Goddess of the South.

Illustration 22 - Canopic Jars
All images by kind permission of Durham University's Oriental Museum
and scanned from my book 'Durham University's Oriental Mummies'

These 'operations' were performed only by priests, each of whom had a specific job, and by the 4th Dynasty, the procedure had developed but had not yet been perfected.

The corpse was initially cleansed with palm wine, various spices, and myrrh, following which it would be covered with natron and left to desiccate for the standard seventy days, although a shorter period has been proposed for the actual desiccation. The desiccated body would then be cleansed again and wrapped in strips of linen, forming the mummy shape. Where the upper classes were concerned, many amulets would be inserted between the layers of wrapping. These were for protection and amongst others included a Heart Scarab, Ankh and Eye of Horus. Many amulets have been discovered in tombs and with mummies during excavations, but there are also many which have been stolen by thieves. Spells derived from Pyramid texts later written on coffins and which were then later written on papyrus scrolls, should the person be rich enough to afford such a papyrus. This was placed in the coffin with the mummy, in the hope the person would enjoy an eternal existence.

Illustration 23 - types of protective amulets, Scarab, Ankh and Eye of Horus
(Author's amulets)

Coffins were normally beautifully decorated with protective gods and goddesses. The colours were symbolic as well as being aesthetic and represented the following:-

> Green was for new life
> Red for life and victory
> White represented purity and omnipotence
> Black had opposite meanings – death and night, life and fertility
> Blue signified water, life and rebirth
> Yellow meant eternal and imperishable

Obviously only the elite could afford such elaborate mummification and these coffins, because as we have seen, this is a very expensive procedure. Not only was the coffin brightly decorated, but also the deceased's facial mask and body covering, which can be seen from these images. Gold was the flesh of the gods, and facial masks were coloured thus for eternal life and to be associated with the deities in death.

Image 24 - Mummy Full mask 25 - unknown lady facial mask 26 - Lady breastplate
All images by kind permission of Durham University's Oriental Museum
and scanned from my book 'Durham University's Oriental Mummies'

The lower classes would merely have cedar oil syringed into the intestines and a plug inserted to prevent leakage. After the period covered in natron, the oil and entrails were removed. These people would not have the privilege of a grand burial, though they would have the comfort of a coffin and would take a few personal items with them to the grave.

Lastly, for the very poor, the cheapest mummification process involved the injection of a purgative, the body being covered with natron and left for the seventy days before being returned to the family. These poor individuals would only have a couple of items interred with them and possibly an amulet in the hope that this would suffice. They may not even have the comfort of a coffin, merely being place directly into the earth.

Although the cheaper forms of mummification were not as elaborate as the richer Egyptians could afford, they still went through the process, including the ritual prayers and offerings, which enabled them to enter the afterlife, should their heart weigh true.

Nevertheless, not all souls reached this idyllic state, such as those who had led an evil life, or committed wicked deeds. Criminals who suffered the death penalty and mutilation, lost all prospect of eternal life according to ancient Egyptian belief.

Prior to entering eternity, many tests had to be passed to enter the Hall of Judgement, where Osiris presided. The richly embalmed people were prepared for this journey, taking with them their protective amulets, and might be provided with scrolls with written advice on how to overcome the numerous malevolent forces.

Essential for the deceased was spell 22 which states the '*Opening of the Mouth*' ceremony in order that they might speak once more. This enabled them to utter the various rituals involved, such as naming the demons blocking entry to a variety of gates through to the underworld. In the Negative Confession, the deceased was expected to name each of the forty-two assessor gods, along with denying his guilt of a specific act of wrong-doing to each deity, as written in spell 125. These and other spells are seen, among others, in the papyri of Nu, the steward of the keeper of the seal and Ani, a Theban scribe and on the coffin inscriptions of Pasenhor, a member of the Libyan Meshwesh. A poignant scene depicts Pasenhor carrying his heart, whilst Thoth leads him to Osiris and an inscription reads 'coming in peace to the beautiful west'[26]. This scene would follow the weighing of the heart of Pasenhor, when Thoth wrote his declaration saying the heart was pure, and found to be devoid of sin. Once a person was led by Anubis to the afterlife, they were then referred to as 'True of Voice' (M3^c ḥrw), and this would be inscribed on stela, tombs and coffins, mainly belonging to the elite.

Unfortunately, for the majority, these procedures were only available to a very small percentage of the population. Once again, these were too expensive for the lower classes.

---

26   Taylor, John, *Spells For Eternity, The Egyptian Book of the Dead*, British Museum Press, London, 2010, 96

The 'Heart Scarab' amulet, which was a symbol of new life and resurrection, as previously noted, was inscribed with Spell 30B from the Book of the Dead:-

> *"my heart…… do not stand up as a witness against me, do not be opposed to me in the tribunal…… in the presence of the Keeper of the Balance!"* [27]

The scarab would be placed under the bandages on the chest in the area of the heart in readiness for its weighing.

Poorer mortals relied purely on perhaps an Ankh or an Eye of Horus amulet, with possibly a clay Heart Scarab and a pre-written magical papyrus scroll, where only their name needed to be inserted. Their journey would be far more treacherous than that of the Pharaoh or a noble.

---

27 Taylor, John, *Death & The Afterlife in Ancient Egypt*, British Museum Press, London, 2001, 18 Taylor, John, *Spells For Eternity, The Egyptian Book of the Dead*, British Museum Press, London, 2010,

CHAPTER SEVEN

Summary of the Evidence of
Law and Punishments

As we have seen, many aspects come into the concept of law and order. It is not as simple as merely behaving oneself, the law of Maat consisted of consideration about life at home, the treatment of others, religion, and avoiding disrupting the cosmic balance amongst other things. Everything had to be taken into account and the Egyptian law structure began with Pharaoh who represented the justice of the gods and anything written or spoken with reference to Pharaoh always had L.P.H. (life, prosperity, health) attached to his name. His right-hand man was his vizier who appointed magistrates, nomarchs (governors of their various nomes or regions) and stewards.

The courts to which felons and disputes were taken included the 'Seru' the initial court of justice, made up of the elders in rural areas, next there were the Kenbets which were regional and national courts and finally the Djadjat, the Royal Court. If a problem could not be solved in the Seru, then it was transferred to the Kenbet. If there was still no satisfaction, then the Djadjat became involved.[28] This was the highest court in Egypt

---

28   https://www.ancient.eu/Egyptian_law

and the men who sat in any court listening to petitions etc., were required to be knowledgeable in all areas.

In the tomb of Rekhmire[29] (TT100 Sheikh Abd el-Qurna, Valley of the Nobles), an 18th Dynasty official under the rule of both Tuthmosis III and Amenhotep II, there are writings on how a vizier behaves, how he relates to other officials, his duties and how to conduct himself according to the law. The official must listen to the petitioner and his judgements must be fair. Should the official make a mistake, his errors must be reported to the clerk.

Edicts such as that of Horemheb, which is the largest extant Law Code states, amongst other things, that in the case of the robbery of a poor man's goods the perpetrator's nose will be cut off, then he will be exiled to Thura, and that officials committing extortion or theft shall suffer the same penalty[30].

Should a slave be taken away from their master or mistress unlawfully, then the same shall befall those who took or kidnapped them.

Abuse or stealing from the population by any soldier results in 100 blows, five open wounds and removal of the stolen items from the person committing the crime. Would they survive this harsh penalty, and if so, would they be accepted back into the army or would they be 'jobless'?

As for judges or any law enforcer, if they falsely accuse another they are committing a capital crime, punishable by death in many cases. Although we have seen that Amenpanufer was guilty of grave robbing, the law enforcers did plant objects to secure a guilty verdict. Eventually, they were also caught and suffered the penalty of death for committing this

---

29   https://www.osirisnet.net/tombes/nobles/rekhmire100/e_rekhmire100_01.htm
30   http://www.touregypt.net/edictofhoremheb.htm

capital crime. Officials are also not allowed to accept gifts as this could be construed as bribery, the same laws of accepting gifts apply today in our society.

Since the body was required to be whole in order to enter eternity, what happened to those who were executed, what would happen if there was no heart to weigh?

An impaled or burnt prisoner had no prepared body to take to eternity, and no heart scarab to assist them. What then was the fate of these grave robbers, murderers and criminals who had suffered the death penalty because of their deeds? Were they taken by the animals and demons before they reached the Hall of Judgement? If by magic they managed to pass the tests, was it certain that the heart would weigh heavy against the feather of Maat, should they still possess one, and would Ammit devour it, causing the victim to "die the second death?" Are these the entities we surmise to be ghosts forever trapped as a non-entity unable to move on, who returned to earth as ghosts, sometimes tormenting the living?

In Amenpanufer's case, this would seem to be the likely outcome. He could not be mummified, was unable to be buried, and had no prayers or amulets for protection through to the Hall of Judgement should he even get that far. And what about Pentewere? Here we have a man who is wrapped in animal skin, partially mummified, buried without a name, who died by apparently taking poison and was discovered in a cache containing royal mummies. There were no amulets, or a papyrus scroll discovered with his body, therefore once again, although of noble birth, he had no protection to guide him to eternity.

Spell 178 from the Book of the Dead[31] suggests death is a gateway to a new life – the afterlife. Even though the Egyptians had this belief, they still had a fear of death, or more likely they feared, as most people do, the unknown.

Even prior to the emergence of Egyptian dynasties, death was considered a new beginning. As previously stated, the predynastic mummy known as 'Gebelein man', c.3400 was discovered buried in the earth along with items from his daily life, and he was discovered in a naturally mummified form. He was also known as 'Ginger' due to the colour of his hair, which was still on his skull.

The deceased to continue in the afterlife required sustenance, and without this they would not survive, hence the need for maintaining the body through mummification, the request to have their names spoken and nourishment to be left at the tomb entrance.

As this was not always feasible, tombs were painted with food and drink, the deceased being depicted before an offering table piled with diverse forms of food. These food offerings were known as 'for the ka of – n k3 n 𓎛 , followed by the deceased's name.

The ancient Egyptian concept of the afterlife depended upon the individual leading an honest life. When eventually the departed arrived to face the final test and his heart was put on the scales, then, it was presumed, the heart scarab would protect him, even if he had done wrong, whether he was rich or poor. Those who had been executed by state executioners or ordered to commit suicide, did not have the same

---

31 Taylor, John, *Death & The Afterlife in Ancient Egypt*, British Museum Press, London, 2001, 12

privileges. One would assume that they would become ghosts, wandering throughout eternity, with neither rest nor peace.

Was it worth taking the risks?

Although many details about the law code are unknown, it is clear that there were principles of law throughout ancient Egyptian history, that certain crimes were regarded as serious offences and that there was a scale of punishments which had been determined for particular crimes.

Illustration 27 - Nebamun (a scribe) enjoying his afterlife,
(Author's drawing and painting after a scene in the Tomb of Nebamun)

Illustration 28 - Anubis leading the deceased to the weighing of their
heart, which weighs as being good, Thoth records the verdict and Horus
leads them to Osiris, who is flanked by Isis and Nephthys.
(Author's photograph)

CHAPTER EIGHT

Current Excavations

As we have seen in previous chapters, tomb robbing and breaking the law in ancient Egyptian times came with serious consequences. So, what are the consequences in today's society, and what do we class as tomb robbing? What defines robbery, as opposed to excavating in order to preserve the artefacts of the past?

There is a simple answer, artefacts removed from their environment and sold on the black market for personal profit is theft, and comes with a fine and or imprisonment, unless those responsible are not caught. Even in today's world, there are those who come across ancient relics and do not hand them in to the authorities, and there are those who know of a place where they can steal items and use them as an extra source of income.

Some would say that Egyptologists who enter a tomb and remove its contents are practising tomb robbery. However, in thinking about this, they are involved in archaeological and scientific investigation and do not steal the items, which are placed in museums where the objects are on the whole, safe from vandals, thieves and black marketeers.

In more recent times there have been many 'digs' enabling Egyptologists, scholars and historians to learn more about Egypt's past and her people.

The Egyptologists of today, are not like many of those of the past, where entering a tomb, royal or otherwise, became a 'free for all'. All aspects of the excavations are undertaken with great care, when removing mummies and their worldly goods and all artefacts are carefully cleaned, labelled and packaged to avoid damage in transit. Once in the museum conservators ensure each item is preserved with some on display, whilst others are in storage, occasionally being brought out for show.

Although money may be exchanged to view the artefacts in museums, this goes towards the upkeep of the place in which they are housed, and for the wages of the people who work there, such as curators, guides, conservators and researchers who enable the public to view what they would be unable to see if the items had not been brought up out of the ground.

Not all previous Egyptologists were careless excavators, and a careful one was Ernesto Schiaparelli who discovered the tomb of Kha and his wife Meryt (TT8). This was the tomb of a noble, Kha, who was a royal architect during the 18th Dynasty and his tomb in the workers' village of Deir el-Medina was found intact. Amongst its contents, foods such as duck, fruit and seeds were discovered along with everyday items including beds, jars, pots, bowls and chests and other items. At the time Arthur Weigall was the Inspector of Antiquities and he accompanied Schiaparelli to the opening of the tomb in 1906 AD.

In various areas many jars containing embalming materials have been found, providing evidence regarding the substances used in the process.

In the necropolis of Abusir a burial shaft hewn into the rocks revealed birds, pots and wooden coffins although these were in bad condition.

In Upper Egypt at Aswan, an excavation team discovered 40 tombs, a scarab which bears the name of Tuthmosis III (considered Egypt's Napoleon) in a cartouche.

Mummies and coffins of the Graeco-Roman and Ptolemaic eras have been discovered recently, some of which are in good condition and others which have not fared so well.

From the New Kingdom reigns of Tuthmosis III and Amenhotep II, rock cut tombs have been discovered along with three rock cut crypts. In the tombs were found animal mummies and three buried infants.

Last but not least we once again come to the tomb of Tutankhamun (KV 62), where radar scans were used to check for hidden rooms behind his burial chamber. The jury is still out on this one, with some Egyptologists not being convinced whether there is anything there or not.

Howard Carter initially went to Egypt in 1891 at the suggestion of Lord and Lady Amherst (known for the Amherst Papyrus, dealing with court transcripts of tomb robberies), who were impressed with his artistic skills. Carter drew tomb reliefs and painted water colours at Beni Hasan for the Egypt Exploration Fund, founded by Amelia Edwards in 1882. He then went on to Deir el-Bersheh, a governors' cemetery of the Eleventh and Twelfth Dynasties.

Early the next year, 1892, Carter met Flinders Petrie in Cairo and worked with him at his excavations in Amarna, Akhenaten's new capitol.

In 1899 Carter was then introduced to a wealthy American Theodore M. Davis, and in 1902 Davis was given permission to work in the Valley of the Kings. By this time Carter was Inspector of Antiquities, and as such, supervised the work. Five years later in 1907-8, Davis discovered sealed pottery jars, linen and floral wreaths. These were examined by Herbert Winlock of the Metropolitan Museum in New York, who informed Carter they appeared to be funerary materials from Tutankhamun's burial. Davis also discovered a faience cup which bore Tutankhamun's name and his name on gold foil. Carter also knew that Tutankhamun's name was originally Tutankhaten before becoming pharaoh, and that he had abandoned Amarna and returned to Thebes where he undertook building works and temple restoration.

Edward R. Ayrton who was working for Davis discovered KV55 in 1907, a tomb which he presumed to be that of Queen Tiye, Akhenaten's mother, but the mummy was that of a young man, many of whom believe is Akhenaten. This has caused much debate amongst academics.

At the same time as Davis was excavating in 1907, Carter began work with Lord Carnarvon in Thebes, and eventually obtained permission to excavate in the Valley of the Kings in 1914. Due to the First World War, work stopped and only resumed in 1917, and thus before the end of the war in the following year. Carter was also aware of the work of a German expedition from 1911-1914 at Amarna during which the now famous head of Nefertiti, Akhenaten's queen, was discovered. With all these discoveries relating to Tutankhamun, Carter was determined to find the tomb, and as we know, after years of searching, the tomb (KV62) was eventually discovered[32].

As we know, the Egyptians wished to be buried where they could rest in peace without being robbed, and to have their names remembered for eternity. Without the work of archaeologists like Howard Carter and others, many would not be known, their names forgotten, unable to live in eternity, except for those who are identified via stela, temples and written works. Those who had suffered '*damnatio memoriae*', such as the above Tutankhamun and his father Akhenaten, they would possibly be unknown or little known if it wasn't for Egyptologists.

---

32 Information on Howard Carter's career comes from personal consultation with Angela Thomas.

In 1862, an American collector named Edwin Smith purchased a papyrus at Luxor from a local dealer which deals with ancient Egyptian medical trauma problems. These include trepanation where a hole or holes are drilled into the skull to relieve pressure on the brain due to a blood clot or swelling etc., injuries, fractures, wounds, dislocations and tumours (cancerous or otherwise). Aspects of our modern medicine via Greek and Roman sources could possibly have been learned from these and other medical papyri from ancient Egypt.

More recently discoveries have been reported from Saqqara, where in December 2018 a 4,400-year-old tomb of a royal priest named Wahtye was opened, he is buried with his wife, mother and other family members. The tomb is beautifully decorated with hieroglyphs, wall paintings and statues.

It is quite a large rock cut tomb measuring 33 feet long x 9 feet 8 inches wide and just under 9 feet high[33].

Following this discovery, just under one year later in October 2019 it was reported at Hatshepsut's Temple at Deir el-Bahri that thirty coffins containing the bodies of men, women and children had been discovered at the Asasif necropolis. The coffins were beautifully decorated and in good condition, dating to Dynasty 22. Decoration included scenes from the Book of the Dead, designs, deities and hieroglyphs. The coffin carvings identified the gender of the deceased by their hands. Females were shown with open hands and the men with clenched fists, and the coffins will be displayed in the new Cairo museum. It has been stated that finding a child's coffin and remains is very rare[34].

33 www.nationalgeographic.com/culture/2018/12/relief-statues-discovered-priest-r...
34 https://www.bbc.co.uk/newsround/50124030

In 2020 it was reported that thirteen intact coffins had been found at Saqqara, thus discoveries continue to be made.

One of my favourite tombs was discovered by Professor Pierre Montet at Tanis and is the burial of Psusennes I, who had an inner anthropoid coffin of silver and funerary mask of gold. Unfortunately, as the intact tomb was discovered early in 1940 it did not receive the publicity it deserved. In the opinion of the author, this tomb is as good a find as Tutankhamun, and the treasure deserves more credit than it has been given.

Another tomb which has yet to be discovered is that of Imhotep, vizier to pharaoh Djoser and builder of the step pyramid. Not only was Imhotep a vizier and builder, he had a great knowledge of medicine and was also a high priest. He was, unusual for anyone but pharaoh, deified after his death. This is one burial the author is hoping will be discovered.

History is learned by studying items from the past including burials. For archaeologists to remove objects in order to ensure their security from thieves is far better than having tombs ransacked, items broken, and either kept for personal use or as previously stated sold for profit.

What would we know of our past and the wonders of the world if such archaeological expeditions had not taken place?

INDEX

A

C

N

Q

R

CARTOUCHES AND HIEROGLYPHS

Note: It is usual for the prenomen or coronation name to follow Pharaoh's title

King of Upper and Lower Egypt (nswt bity), followed by his birth name in the second cartouche, which is preceded in most cases by Sa Re, (Son of Re). For example,

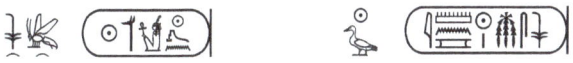

nswt bity UserMaatre Setepenre, Sa Re Ramessu Meryamun - Ramesses II (the great)

Illustration 29 - Karnak Temple Hieroglyphs of Ramesses II
(Author's photograph)

Most Pharaohs' names have Greek alternatives, and in the cases of Tuthmosis I, II, III and IV, we know them through these Greek versions of Tuthmosis. Their Egyptian names are Djehutymes I, II, III and IV, and pharaoh [pr c3 ⬚ *pr*] means Great House.

PHARAOHS

Akhenaten
(Neferkheperure)

Amenemhat I
(Sehetepibre)

Amenemhat III
(NyMaatre)

Amenhotep II (Heqa Iunu)
Akheperure

Amenhotep III Heqa Waset
(NebMaatre)

Djoser
(Netjerikhet)

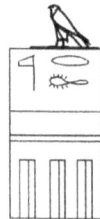

Khafre

Khufu

Merenptah HetepherMaat,
(Baenre-merynetjeru)

Narmer

Nebkaure Akhtoy

Pepi I Meryre

Psusennes I
Pasebakhaenniut I, mry
Imn, (beloved of Amun)
Akheperre Setepenamun,
(chosen of Amun)

Ramesses I Menpehtyre

Ramesses II (the great) Meryamun, (UserMaatre Setepenre)

Ramesses III Heqa Iunu, (UserMaatre MeryAmun)

Ramesses IV (HeqaMaatre)

Ramesses VI (NebMaatre Meryamun), Epithet, Amun-hir-khopsh-ef-Netjer-Heqa Iunu

Ramesses IX (Neferkhare Setepenre), Epithet Kha-em-waset Mery-Amun

Senusret, Sesostris I, (Kheperkare)

Seqenenre Tao (qen) II

Seti I, Meryenptah (MenMaatre)

Seti II Merenptah, (Userkheperure-setepenre)

Siptah (Akhenre-Setepenre Merenptah)

Smendes I Nesbanebdjed
Mery-Amun, (Hedjkheperre
Setepenre)

Sobekemsaf II, (Sekhemre
Shedtawy)

Sobekhotep II Amenemhet
VI, (Sekhemre Khutaway)

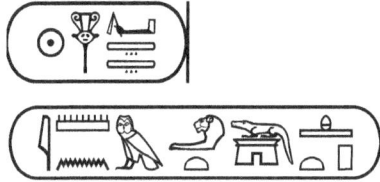

Teti I

Tutankhamun
Heqa Iunu Shema (Ruler
of Southern On, i.e.
Thebes)
Nebkheperure

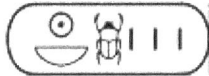

Tuthmosis III
(Menkheperre)

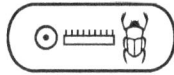

Userkare

QUEENS

Hatshepsut,
Queen/king, (Maatkare)

Nefertiti

Tiye (minor wife of
Ramesses III)

(Weret-Imtes) "Great of
sceptre"

ROYAL SONS AND DAUGHTERS

Henutmire (Ramesses II's
Daughter)

Pentewere (son of Tiye &
Ramesses III)

GODS AND GODDESSES

Amun-Re

Anubis/
Inpu

Horus

Isis

Khepri

Khnum

Maat

Nephthys

Osiris

Re

Re Horakhty

Thoth (Ḏhwty)

Nobels, Scribes and Sages

Amennakhte, scribe

Ani, Theban scribe

Ankhtifi, a noble

Harshire, a scribe

Ipuwer, Egyptian Sage

Khapmope, a scribe

Nesamun, royal scribe

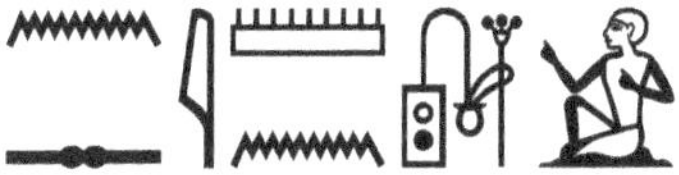

VIZERS AND COURT OFFICIALS

Hezi (vizier to king Teti I)

Imhotep (vizier)

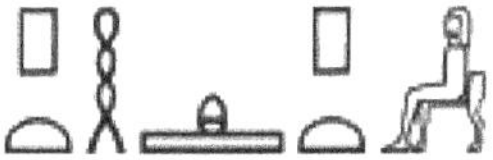

Irinufer, (TT290, Servant in the Place of Truth, sḏm cš m st m3ct)

Kha, (TT8, royal architect)

Khaemwese, a vizier

Nu, Steward of the Keeper
of the Seal

Ptahhotep, a vizier

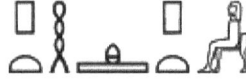

Weni (court official

VARIOUS HIEROGLYPHS

Ba

Blessed Dead Revered One,
True of Voice (im3ḫw m3c
ḥrw)

Egypt (Kemet)

God, ntr

Ka

For the Ka of

King of Upper and Lower
Egypt, Nswt bity

Lord of the two lands, nb
t3wy

Son of Re, S3 Re

True of voice, Maat ḥrw

BIBLIOGRAPHY

Atkinson, B. A. *Durham University's Oriental Museum Mummies.* UK Book Publishing: Whitley Bay 2019.

Clayton, P. A. *Chronicle of the Pharaohs, The Reign by Reign Record of the Rulers and Dynasties of Ancient Egypt.* Thames and Hudson: London 1994, 2006.

Dodson A. and Hilton D. *The Complete Royal Families of Ancient Egypt.* Thames and Hudson: London 2004.

Gahlin, Lucia. *Egypt, Gods, Myths and Religion.* Lorenz Books, an imprint of Anness Publishing Ltd: London 2001, 2007.

Gill, A. *Ancient Egyptians: The Kingdom of the Pharaohs Brought to Life.* Harper Collins Entertainment, an imprint of Harper Collins Publishers: London 2003, 2004.

Laurén, G. (ed.) *The Historical Library of Diodorus the Sicilian in Forty Books, Volume 1, Books 1-14.* Sophron Editor 2014.

Lichtheim, M. *Ancient Egyptian Literature, The Old and Middle Kingdoms.* Vol. 1. University of California Press: Berkeley and Los Angeles 1973.

Lichtheim, M. *Ancient Egyptian Literature, The New Kingdom.* Vol. II., University of California Press: Berkeley and Los Angeles 1976.

Mee, A. *The Children's Encyclopaedia*. Vol. 1A, Everybody's Publications Ltd., The Educational Book Company: London 1963.

Smith, G. E. *The Royal Mummies*. Imprimerie de l'Institut Français d'Archéologie Orientale: Cairo 1912, Reprinted Gerald Duckworth & Co. Ltd: London 2000.

Taylor, John. *Spells for Eternity, The Ancient Egyptian Book of the Dead*, British Museum Press: London 2010.

Taylor, John. *Death and the Afterlife in Ancient Egypt*, British Museum Press: London 2001.

Tyldesley J. *Daughters of Isis*. Viking Books: London 1994, 1995.

Tyldesley, J. *The Pharaohs*. Quercus Publishing Plc: London 2009.

Wilkinson, R. H. *The Complete Gods and Goddesses of Ancient Egypt*. Thames and Hudson: London 2003.

FURTHER READING

Aldred, C. *Egyptian Art in the Days of the Pharaohs 3100-320BC*. Thames and Hudson World of Art: London 1980.

Dewald. C. (ed.), Waterfield, R. (translator). *Herodotus, The Histories*. Oxford University Press: Oxford 2008.

Faulkner, R.O. *A Concise Dictionary of Middle Egyptian*. Griffith Institute: Oxford 1962, 2009.

Gardiner, A (Sir). *Egypt of the Pharaohs.* Oxford University Press: Oxford 1961, 1964

Johnson, K. L. & Petty, B. *The Names of the Kings of Egypt, The Serekhs and Cartouches of Egypt's Pharaohs, along with selected Queens.* Museum Tours Press: Littleton, USA 2012.

Oakes, L. *Sacred Sites of Ancient Egypt: An Illustrated Guide to the Temples and Tombs of the Pharaohs.* Hermes House, an imprint of Anness Publishers Ltd: London 2001, 2003.

Pemberton, D. *Treasures of the Pharaohs: The Glories of Ancient Egypt.* Duncan Baird Publishers Ltd: London 2004.

Petty, B. *Egyptian Glyphary: A Sign List Based Hieroglyphic Dictionary of Middle Egyptian.* Museum Tours Press, a division of Museum Tours Inc: Littleton, USA 2012.

Quirke, S. *Who Were the Pharaohs? A History of their names with a list of cartouches.* British Museum Publications Ltd: London 1990.

Shaw, I. and Nicholson, P.(eds.) *The British Museum Dictionary of Ancient Egypt.* The British Museum Press: London 2002.

Tyldesley, J. *Egypt: How a Lost Civilisation was Rediscovered.* BBC Books, an imprint on Ebury Publishers: London 2005, 2006, 2008.

Tyldesley, J. *Judgement of the Pharaoh: Crime and Punishment in Ancient Egypt.* Phoenix, an imprint of Orion Books Ltd: London 2001.

OTHER SOURCES

Researched on various dates and on more than one occasion, therefore dates have not been included.

1. http://www.deirelmedina.com/lenka/TurinKha.html

2. https://osirisnet.net/tombes/nobles/amenemhat82/e_amenem-hat82_06.htm

3. http://www.touregypt.net/featurestories/cache.htm

4. http://www.thewisemag.com/mystery/the-magic-of-mandrake

5. https://www.osirisnet.net/tombes/nobles/rekhmire100/e_rekhmire100_01.htm

6. http://www.touregypt.net/edictofhoremheb.htm

Jsesh Hieroglyphic Editor - used for the hieroglyphs contained in this book